Maritime Salvage Operati‹
Environmental Protection

This book questions the use of salvage law as legal regulatory framework for the remuneration of environmental services in salvage operations, proposing that such services should be based on direct contracting between commercial salvors and coastal States. Adopting an environment-first approach, it argues that direct contracting better serves and promotes environmental protection outcomes. It also takes a functional view of the law as a tool to promote values and sought outcomes. Salvage operations are recognised as the first line of defence against pollution following shipping incidents. Although regulated under the law of salvage, these operations form an integral component of a framework of environmental protection measures regulated under different legal instruments or laws. The law of salvage fails to effectively integrate salvage operations into broader pollution response mechanisms because it does not align comfortably with this framework of laws. Despite the emphasis on environmental protection in the 1989 London Salvage Convention, the Convention maintains the traditional notion of salvage operations as a service to property, while environmental outcomes and the remuneration of environmental services are positioned as a secondary outcome of the law of salvage. This book argues that directly contracting for environmental services bolsters the primacy of environmental protection and the functional use of law to further environmental protection and policy formulation. Direct contracting between coastal States and salvors for environmental services complements existing practices and pollution response mechanisms and provides a sound legal basis for the effective realisation of salvage operations as the first line of defence against pollution following shipping incidents without fundamentally altering the established commercial identity of the traditional law of salvage. This book will be key reading for students, academics, and practitioners working at the intersection of shipping and environmental law.

Durand M Cupido is Lecturer in Law at the University of Essex, UK, and a qualified attorney of the High Court of South Africa (non-practising). Durand has practised as a commercial litigation attorney and continues to advise on maritime law and related matters.

Routledge Research on the Law of the Sea

Maritime Salvage Operations and Environmental Protection

Durand M Cupido

Routledge
Taylor & Francis Group

LONDON AND NEW YORK

First published 2023
by Routledge
4 Park Square, Milton Park, Abingdon, Oxon OX14 4RN

and by Routledge
605 Third Avenue, New York, NY 10158

Routledge is an imprint of the Taylor & Francis Group, an informa business

British Library Cataloguing-in-Publication Data
A catalogue record for this book is available from the British Library

ISBN: 978-1-032-32534-7 (hbk)
ISBN: 978-1-032-32535-4 (pbk)
ISBN: 978-1-003-31550-6 (ebk)

DOI: 10.4324/9781003315506

Typeset in Times New Roman
by Deanta Global Publishing Services, Chennai, India

I dedicate this book to my little man (at least for now), James Martin Cupido.

Contents

Acknowledgements

I wish to thank Mr Stan Woznicki, Head of Counter Pollution & Salvage, at the United Kingdom's Maritime & Coastguard Agency, and Mr Graham Caldwell, the Receiver of Wreck at the Maritime & Coastguard Agency (MCA). I could tap into their considerable knowhow, and they patiently answered my many questions. I am further indebted to MCA Counter Pollution & Salvage for giving me insight into the relevant contractual arrangements with tug owners for the provision of services aimed at the protection of the UK coastline.

I must also thank Thomas Miller P&I Ltd, and Donjon-Smit Salvage, for giving me their blessings to discuss the Donjon-Smit LLC, OPA 1990, Salvage, Firefighting, and Lightering Contract and Funding Agreement.

Last but not least, I wish to thank Professor Onyeka Osuji for reading through drafts of this work and for his invaluable advice. Of course, any remaining mistakes and/or omissions are my own.

Introduction

Maritime salvage operations are defined as acts or activities undertaken 'to assist a vessel or any other property in danger in navigable waters'.[1] However, these same operations are also recognised as a first line of defence against pollution following shipping incidents and an important component in a broader environmental protection framework.[2] This second aspect of salvage operations has and continues to underpin demands for changes to the law of salvage that traditionally pertained to the safeguarding of property at sea.[3] Changes to the law of salvage to pursue environmental protection outcomes in the context of salvage operations, described as 'the greening of salvage law',[4] came via the 1989 London Salvage Convention.[5] The key, albeit not only, change came in the form of added financial incentives[6] for salvors to encourage them to respond to maritime casualties involving a threat to the environment.

The choice of salvage law as the regulatory framework for the remuneration of salvors' environmental services in salvage operations involved the assumption that this area of the law and the Salvage Convention was

---

1 The International Convention on Salvage 1989, Article 1(a).
2 See discussion below, p 70 ff.
3 See below (n 10).
4 Hedman S 'Expressive Functions of Criminal Sanctions in Environmental Law' (1990–1991) 59 *Geo. Wash. L. Rev.* 889.
5 A reading of the Convention (see discussion in Chapter 5) shows that the Convention is expressive of environmental protection values, both in its statement of purpose in the pre-amble and the way the substantive provisions appear to be drafted in furtherance of this purpose. See also generally *Semco Salvage and Marine Pte Ltd v Lancer Navigation Co Ltd The Nagasaki Spirit* [1997] 1 All ER 502, where Lord Mustill, with reference to the preamble of the convention, accepted submissions made by the late Geoffrey Brice, that the explicit purpose of the Convention was 'to provide "adequate incentives" to keep [salvors] in readiness to protect the environment'. At 512. *Emphasis added.*
6 See discussion of Articles 13 and 14 of the Convention in Chapter 5, 45 *ff.*

DOI: 10.4324/9781003315506-1

appropriate for this purpose. Moreover, this greening of salvage took place despite other viable options for remuneration outside of the law of salvage that were potentially better suited to the promotion of environmental protection outcomes.[7] These remuneration possibilities include those under international instruments such as the 1992 International Convention of Civil Liability for Oil Pollution Damage, the 1992 Fund Conventions, and more recent instruments such as the International Convention on Civil Liability for Bunker Oil Pollution Damage, 2001, and The Hazardous and Noxious Substances Convention, 1996 and a 2010 protocol to it. The latter two have not yet entered into force. Very importantly, one may also add contractual arrangements between salvors and coastal States directed at pollution prevention in the case of shipping incidents[8] to these instruments.

This study questions the choice of the law of salvage and continued demands for further changes to the private law of salvage in response to the growing, broader social interest in environmental protection. It takes the position that the remuneration of environmental services does not fully align with the historical development of the law of salvage as a service to maritime property interests for reward, in furtherance of marine commerce.[9] Insisting on such changes, given viable alternatives outside of the law of salvage, results in the questionable and unnecessary fragmentation of legal avenues for remuneration.

Nevertheless, discussions regarding the possible amendment of the Convention or even its replacement have persisted,[10] as evidenced by attempts of the ISU[11] to have 'environmental awards' incorporated into

---

7 See discussion of instruments of remuneration outside of salvage in Chapter 5, 81 *ff.*

8 Retainer contracts between coastal States and professional salvors is a growing phenomenon.

9 See discussion on the theory of salvage in Chapter 3, 31.

10 In this regard, the Comite Maritime International CMI) Argentine MLA Colloquium held in October 2010, saw numerous proposals by, among others, the International Salvage Union (ISU), the London Property Underwriters, International P&I Clubs, and the International Chamber of Shipping (ICS), on questions pertaining to the possible amendment of the 1989 Salvage Convention. Documents pertaining to the discussions can be accessed at the CMI website, www.comitemaritime.org/Salvage-Convention-1989/0,2746,14632,00.html accessed 27 September 2021.

11 The International Salvage Union (ISU), an association of professional salvors, are at the forefront of calls for the remuneration of salvors that recognises the practical role of salvors in marine environmental protection. The primary role of the ISU is to represent, promote and safeguard the interests of member salvors in legal, political and commercial arenas. Beyond acting as an effective lobbying organisation for the salvage industry, the ISU also works to foster co-operation between members. As a lobbying organisation for the salvage industry, the The ISU has played an important role in many legal and commercial developments concerning marine salvage. It is a member of the Lloyd's Salvage Group and also

the law of salvage.[12] These efforts, which include suggestions to introduce environmental salvage awards into the fabric of property salvage, have been unsuccessful. At the 40th Conference of the Comité Maritime International (CMI) for the review of the International Salvage Convention held in Beijing in October 2012, proposals for the introduction of a new environmental salvage award were not accepted and indications are that 'it [is] unlikely that the Salvage Convention will be amended to include environmental salvage in the foreseeable future'.[13] Possible explanations for this might include the difficulty of formally incorporating the relatively recent broader social interest in environmental protection into an area of law shaped in a commercial property context with a significant focus on private interests. For this reason, this study deviates from an approach that has almost exclusively looked within the framework of the private law of salvage to address the question of the remuneration of environmental services in salvage operations.

This deviation is informed by the reality of a change in value systems that has seen environmental protection concerns become paramount within the broader discourse of sustainable development and legal development generally. Should one accept the view of the law as a tool to realise sought values or outcomes,[14] then one must acknowledge that such a change in value systems would necessarily impact upon any discussion pertaining to legal development. In relation to the law of salvage, it is likely that those primarily interested in environmental protection (this study will employ the term environmentalists when referring to these interests) would assign different priorities as between the traditional property rescue objectives of

---

has observer status at the International Maritime Organization and the International Oil Pollution Compensation Fund. For further information on the ISU, see www.marine-salvage.com accessed on 24 March 2022.

12 The notion of environmental awards, if one is to accept that better awards will encourage salvors to engage in environmental services, is certainly gaining popularity. The ISU, in pushing for reviews on how salvors are rewarded, are particularly partial to the notion of "environmental awards". Thus, they are pushing for a reward which would not only award them for services to ship and cargo, but also their efforts and success in preventing damage to the environment. In this regard, also see the speech delivered by Mr Todd Busch at the CMI Argentine MLA Colloquium held during October 2010. The pdf document of this speech can be accessed at www.comitemaritime.org/Salvage-Convention-1989/0 ,2746,14632,00.html accessed 27 September 2021. Also see King J, *Salvage: Bringing the Environment on Board* Unpublished LLM Thesis (University of Cape Town).

13 'Little support to amend the salvage convention to adopt environmental salvage' *INSIGHT* 209, 2013. www.gard.no/web/updates/content/20734088/little-support-to-amend-the-salvage-convention-to-adopt-environmental-salvage accessed 03 April 2022.

14 See discussion of Roscoe Pound's social interest theory of law below, Chapter 1, p. 9.

salvage and environmental protection. It is also likely that their choice of a legal regulatory framework for the remuneration of environmental services within salvage operations might not necessarily be the law of salvage. This study seeks to account for this point of view in its critique of the law of salvage as the basis for remunerating environmental services.

As such, this study is predicated upon an approach that regards the environment and its protection as a primary concern, i.e., an 'environment-first approach'. It proceeds from an understanding of salvage operations as a functional component in a broader environmental protection framework of laws. Integral to this understanding of salvage operations is the view that the law of salvage in its regulation of such operations should complement rather than detract from this broader system and that salvage operations should be effectively integrated into a broader environmental protection framework.

The chosen approach for this study is based on an idea advanced by the late Professor Barend Van Niekerk, that environmental protection should be a fundamental norm in all spheres of law.[15] Given that Van Niekerk's view amounts to a preference for, or a choice of environmental values relative to other values or interests, the work also draws upon the 'social interest theory' of Roscoe Pound. This theory is predicated upon a functional understanding of the law in which the identification and balancing of private, public, and social interests is paramount.[16] This theory finds good application in modern salvage operations, which have increasingly come to involve the careful balancing of commercial and environmental outcomes. Nevertheless, this approach to the analysis of environmental services in salvage operations has not been a feature of academic writing to date, likely because commercial interests in the form of shipowners, salvors, and their insurers have provided the prominent voices in discussions about environmental services within salvage operations. As such, the legal developmental discourse took place against a decidedly commercial backdrop.

While existing works have typically acknowledged the importance of environmental outcomes for this area of the law, they have not afforded the former a position of priority relative to the private and commercial outcomes of salvage.[17] Absent from existing works is also any attempt at providing an integrated examination of salvage operations within a broader framework of legal instruments potentially applicable to environmental services in

---

15 Van Niekerk 'The Ecological Norm in law or the Jurisprudence of the Fight Against Pollution' 1975 *SALJ* 78

16 See discussion in Chapter 1.

17 See De La Rue C and Anderson B, *Shipping and the Environment* (London, LLP, 1998).

such operations. In this regard, the closest attempt is that of De La Rue and Anderson,[18] who discuss claims by salvors under certain public law instruments such as the 1992 International Convention of Civil Liability for Oil Pollution Damage and the 1992 Fund Conventions. While the authors note the shortcomings of the Salvage Convention in relation to environmental protection aims, they stop short of questioning the fundamental assumption of the credibility of the law of salvage as regulatory vehicle for the remuneration of environmental services. As such, neither De La Rue and Anderson nor any other authors have considered remuneration avenues for environmental services in salvage operations outside of the law of salvage as an actual or exclusive alternative to the law of salvage, grounded on an environment-first approach.

With this environmental-first approach, this work provides an expanded canvass for future legal development. It does this by proposing an alternative approach to the remuneration of salvors for environmental services in the form of contracting between commercial salvors and coastal States. This approach aligns with current practices[19] and addresses the unnecessary fragmentation of avenues for remuneration of environmental services, without detracting from the dual functionality of salvage operations. Moreover, it allows for improved integration of salvage operations into a broader framework of laws tasked with pollution prevention, without fundamentally altering the established commercial property identity of the traditional law of salvage, thereby introducing uncertainty.

The study is divided into six chapters. Chapter 1 provides an overview of Roscoe Pound's theory of interests and its application by the late Professor Barend Van Niekerk in arguing for the adoption of a fundamental ecological norm.[20] This conceptualisation of environmental protection as a fundamental interest and a concern to be balanced against other competing interests serves as the ideal backdrop for the critical examination of the law of salvage and the Convention as a regulatory framework for environmental services in salvage operations.

Chapter 2 provides a historical overview of the development of salvage law and some of the factors that have shaped its development. In line with the idea of legal regulation as the pursuit and balancing of outcomes, this includes the identification of underlying values and policies that have shaped salvage law as a service to property. The historical analysis also

---

18 Ibid.
19 See discussion in Chapter 5 of the use of contracts to implement salvage capability into coastal State pollution response mechanisms.
20 Van Niekerk 1975 *SALJ* 78 (n 15).

demonstrates that, relative to the property and commercial outcomes of salvage, its environmental protection aim is relatively recent. As such, the latter's regulation as part of the law of salvage in furtherance of an environment-first approach may necessitate changes to the law of salvage that are fundamentally at odds with its historical development as a service to property.

Chapter 3 provides a theoretical analysis of salvage law, examining its legal nature and the extent to which its theoretical underpinnings could potentially account for environmental services in salvage operations. Ultimately, the chapter demonstrates that the very theoretical underpinnings of salvage law limit the effective broader pursuit of efficient environmental protection outcomes in salvage operations. These very limitations of the law of salvage to further environmental concerns also triggered the drastic legislative intervention that came in the form of the Salvage Convention. Understanding the limitations of the law of salvage as primary vehicle for addressing environmental concerns and the remuneration of environmental services in salvage operations, especially from an environmentalist perspective, highlights the need to consider other legal alternatives.

Chapter 4 examines the Salvage Convention, which was premised on the furthering of environmental protection outcomes ih an area of the law traditionally not geared towards it. Therefore, it is necessary to examine the instrument as the means employed to address the inherent limitations of salvage law and to assess the way it balances environmental protection and commercial outcomes. In this regard, the chapter shows that the Convention represents an uneasy fusion of public provisions with the private provisions of traditional salvage law in order to address environmental outcomes. The Convention, as it stands, detracts from the broader environmental protection legal framework that consists of both private (contractual) mechanisms and public law instruments that are potentially better able to address public law concerns. This informs the ultimate recommendations of this study that the remuneration of salvors for environmental services is better placed outside of the law of salvage. Instead, such remuneration is better regulated via contracting between coastal States representing the public interests and salvors. Not only does this represent a development that is more in line with current practices, but it also allows for the efficient defragmentation of legal regulatory issues in relation to salvors' remuneration and a broader more orderly template for future legal development. Essentially, in relation to remuneration for environmental services, the Salvage Convention has taken development as far as it can without introducing fundamental changes to an established system of law.

Chapter 5 looks at the recognition and placement of salvage operations within coastal State pollution response mechanisms and examines avenues for remuneration available to salvors outside of the law of salvage. In relation to the former, the chapter examines the recognition of salvage operations and the contractual mechanisms employed to integrate these operations in pollution response mechanisms. This will not only assess the efficacy of current contractual arrangements but also provide the groundwork for suggestions regarding the way forward in relation to the use of contracts to remunerate environmental services.

While contractual relationships between salvors and coastal States are widely used, the study will be restricted to their use in the United Kingdom (UK), which has ratified the Civil Liability and Fund Conventions. The study also includes a reference to the United States of America, as an example of a State outside of the regulatory ambit of these instruments that uses contractual arrangements to integrate salvage services into pollution response measures. This comparison also serves to highlight how, notwithstanding the adoption of its own domestic legislation instead of aligning itself with the international regimes, the jurisdiction also recognises the utility of salvage operations as integral to pollution response mechanisms.

The second part of this chapter also examines possibilities for remuneration outside of salvage under select public instruments, namely the Civil Liability and Fund Conventions. In this regard, the focus is primarily on the alignment and interaction of these instruments with the 1989 Salvage Convention. This chapter demonstrates how the regulation of environmental services in salvage operations under the International Salvage Convention detracts from remuneration possibilities under these public law instruments. Importantly also, it demonstrates how the appropriate use of contracts will allow for a better synthesis of the Salvage Convention and these instruments, while also addressing the unnecessary legal fragmentation of the current system. This will provide not only a more orderly approach to regulating the dual nature of salvage operations but also a fairer system of remuneration.

Chapter 6 contains the primary recommendations of this work, namely, that the remuneration of environmental services in salvage operations is best regulated on the basis of contracts between coastal States and salvors. This represents a novel approach in the academic analysis of salvage operations and the remuneration of environmental services, deviating from an approach that has to date exclusively looked for substantive changes to the law of salvage. It bridges the gap between law and practice, in that pollution prevention agreements with salvors are a reality of coastal States' pollution response efforts, which has not received the required contextual academic scrutiny offered in this study.

Based on the findings in the preceding chapters, this chapter also includes a brief discussion of why the introduction of an award for environmental services in the law of salvage will simply reintroduce the difficulties inherent in pasting public provisions into a private instrument such as the Salvage Convention. Compared to this, the contract-based solution for the remuneration of environmental services in salvage presents a more efficient, legally viable mechanism for the promotion of the social interest in the protection of the environment. As such, the study's ultimate recommendations are based upon solutions already (under)utilised in practice although this has not given rise to attempts to examine the legal theoretical possibilities afforded by these solutions to address the fragmented state of the current legal regulatory framework.

The significance of this study lies in its approach to the standard uncritical assumptions about the law of salvage and its potential reach. It also elevates the environment as an essential stakeholder in the development of commercial law and appropriately positions salvage operations as a functional component in a broader environmental law framework. It does this without detracting from the theoretical framework of the law of salvage, thereby introducing uncertainty, and expands the legal theoretical possibilities for meaningful developments around salvage operations and salvors' remuneration for environmental services.

Bibliography

De La Rue C and Anderson B, *Shipping and the Environment* (LLP, 1998)

Hedman S, 'Expressive Functions of Criminal Sanctions in Environmental Law' (1990–1991) 59 Geo. Wash. L. Rev. 889

Van Niekerk, 'The Ecological Norm in Law or the Jurisprudence of the Fight against Pollution' (1975) 92 SALJ 78

1 Environment First, Pursuing and Balancing of Values Via the Law

This chapter examines and explains the operation and the pursuit of values through law as a conceptual backdrop to the later examination of the law of salvage as legal regulatory choice for the remuneration of salvors' environmental services. This, as will be shown, involves not only the singular choice of a value to be promoted but an appreciation of the balancing exercise often involved where we seek to promote potentially conflicting values. With the aim of reaching a working understanding of the relationship between values and law, this chapter draws on the social interest theory of Roscoe Pound and its application by the late Professor Barend Van Niekerk in arguing for the adoption of a fundamental ecological norm[1] (essentially an environment-first approach). A primary assumption of this work is that Van Niekerk's views regarding environmental protection as a fundamental concern will gain further traction in years to come as environmental protection concerns become more acute.

The chapter commences by setting out Pound's social interest theory. This helps to establish the notion that the choice of a legal regulatory framework is an essential aspect of the pursuit of values via the law. This is then followed by a discussion of Van Niekerk's application of Pound's social interest theory in arguing for the adoption of a fundamental ecological norm.

Pound's Social Interest Theory

Pound emphasises the centrality of values (preferences and demands) to the law and the law as a tool to realise such values.[2] As such, his theory of interests is premised upon a functional understanding of law in which the

---

1 Van Niekerk, 'The Ecological Norm in Law or the Jurisprudence of the Fight Against Pollution' 1975 SALJ 78.
2 Pound R, Social Control through Law (Archon Books, 1968).

DOI: 10.4324/9781003315506-2

attainment of 'demands or desires [values] which humans, either individually or in groups or associations or relations, seek to satisfy' is paramount.[3] In this regard, he has also observed that the satisfaction of 'human claims and demands and desires is constant, not the exact machinery of satisfying them'.[4] This observation is particularly apt when considered against demands for changes to the law of salvage to address environmental protection concerns and, indeed, the very choice of salvage law as legal regulatory framework for salvors' environmental services.

Why should these services be regulated as part of the law of salvage when, as will be shown in later chapters,[5] their regulation is limited by narrow definitions and the historical property and trade bias of salvage law? More so when one considers that viable alternatives might be available. Perhaps the broader social interest in the protection of the environment might be better served outside of the theoretical framework of salvage, rather than insisting on substantive changes to the law of salvage.[6] Of course, while the utility of law in the realisation of values is evident, another undeniable aspect of the law and its function is its role in ensuring social order. In the view of this author, this function can only be properly realised in a system of law that is orderly. For this reason, one must carefully consider the choice of legal regulatory vehicle in the pursuit of values, especially where they may conflict. In making such a choice, one must necessarily be mindful of the primary function of law as a tool for maintaining social order, which demands that the integrity of the system and its internal coherence (order) is maintained.

Pound categorises demands or desires as individual, public, and social interests,[7] with the first two capable of being subsumed under the third, given that the third category entails claims of a 'whole social group'.[8] In situations involving a conflict of demands we necessarily have to engage in a balancing exercise, which is also where the matter of perspective may determine relative priority. However, Pound notes that the balancing or weighing of competing interests must be undertaken 'on the same plane',[9] so that individual interests must be compared with individual and social with social. So, when we consider conflicting interests in 'some new aspect or new situation, it is important to subsume the individual interests under

---

3 Pound R, 'A Survey of Social Interests' (1943), 57 *Harvard LR* 1.
4 Ibid 9.
5 See Chapters 4 and 5.
6 See Introduction, n 12.
7 Pound 57 *Harvard LR* 1 (n 3).
8 Ibid 2.
9 Ibid.

social interests and to weigh them as such'.[10] In the context of salvage this would mean that the individual interests of salvors and shipowners are not the key interests to be balanced against the social interest in environmental protection but rather the broader social interests these may inform. In the case of salvage, these have historically been the advancement of trade and maritime commerce,[11] which also explains the prominent involvement of commercial interests in the development of the Salvage Convention.

Van Niekerk's Fundamental Ecological Norm

As an adherent of Pound's theory of interest and an environmentalist, the views of the late Professor Barend Van Niekerk also provide insight into matters pertaining to the regulation of salvors' remuneration for environmental services.[12] Professor Van Niekerk, drawing on Pound's theory of interests, notes the importance of understanding fundamental jurisprudential and social issues for the law to become 'properly involved in the broad field of the protection of man's environment'.[13] In this sense, in the context of environmental pollution and legal responses thereto, he recognises the conflict between the 'desire ... of [mainly large corporations] to achieve short-term economies or financial advantage and the interest of society at large'.[14] Consistent with the idea of comparison 'on the same plane',[15] he notes that the utilisation of the social theory of law and the balancing of interests would only work if the short-term economic interests are converted into a recognisable social interest.

Van Niekerk's observation has pertinent implications for salvage operations where the operation of individual interests and broader social interests is evident. As mentioned, the obvious individual interests include professional salvors wanting to get paid for their services while property owners have a commercial interest in their property being saved and the minimisation of potential liability. Consistent with the Social Interest Theory, these short-term economic interests can and have been expressed as underpinning a broader social interest in the advancement of trade, commerce, and

---

10 Ibid 3.
11 See discussion of the history of salvage in Chapter 2 (p 16 *ff*) and the theory of salvage in Chapter 3.
12 Van Niekerk, B 1975 *SALJ* 78 (n 1).
13 Ibid 78.
14 Ibid 79.
15 Pound (1943), 57 *Harvard LR* (n 3) 2.

industry.[16] It is this broader social interest that must be balanced against the interest in environmental protection. The idea is that environmental risks are to be tolerated only if the social interests in trade (notwithstanding the individual economic interests) and the development of industries 'substantially outweigh the cost to society (both in the short and in the long term)'.[17]

However, Van Nierkerk adds 'the crucial caveat'[18] that there are instances where 'no advantage, however great, immediate and enduring, would justify ... encroachments on the right of society ... to a pollution-free environment'.[19] He then includes as an example of such an instance the

> use in certain waters of oil tankers of a tonnage so great that a mishap will result in irreparable harm to the natural resources of the area and possibly even the emission into the atmosphere or the sea of certain substances that render life in that area hazardous.[20]

It is in this context that Van Nierkerk identifies the 'fundamental jurisprudential problem of environmental pollution',[21] thus posing the question whether 'recognition cannot be given to a general jurisprudential norm against ecological damage; a norm which would be operative in all fields of the law both national and international – and on all levels of the administration of justice'.[22] Van Niekerk's example of oil tankers and the threats they pose are particularly apposite, given that such incidents also triggered the 'greening of salvage law' and broader public law instruments.[23] This adds to the curiosity that is the absence of more critical 'environment-first' assessments of developments in the law of salvage and ways to effectively promote this interest in salvage operations.

Ultimately, recognising that different legal systems attach greater or lesser degrees of importance to values,[24] he argues that 'protection of the ecology must now be regarded as one of the primary concerns of law'.[25] He then proceeds to argue for the adoption of a fundamental ecological norm applicable in all areas of law, public and private. He suggests that

16 *The Fusilier* (1865) Br. of Lush. 341, 347. See discussion of *The Fusilier* and the public policy underpinnings of salvage in Chapter 3, pp 35–36.
17 Van Niekerk (n 1) 79.
18 Ibid.
19 Ibid.
20 Ibid.
21 Ibid 81.
22 Ibid 82.
23 See discussion in Chapter 2, pp 29–30.
24 Van Niekerk (n 1) 82.
25 Ibid 83.

this fundamental norm 'can be used as the basis for a canon of construction in the interpretation of *all* statutes where the problem of environmental pollution arises'.[26] This will this have implications not only for the law of salvage, which traditionally only considered services to property in furtherance of maritime commerce, but also for the question of the appropriate legal categorisation of services in furtherance of environmental outcomes. For example, accepting the fundamentality of a fundamental ecological norm, one might ask whether the law of salvage is sufficiently reflective of such a norm. One might go further and question the actual choice of salvage law as regulatory framework for salvors' remuneration for environmental services within salvage operations; more so, when considering the historical development of salvage as a service to property and adjunct to trade.[27] Environmental protection in the context of property salvage operations could have been subjected to a legal regulatory regime more acutely directed at environmental protection instead of seeking to effect changes that may ultimately introduce uncertainty into an area of law that was shaped within the context of trade. Therefore, taking an environmentalist approach mindful of the traditional property and commercial bias of salvage law, it is necessary, at least, to explore alternatives to the law of salvage as a regulatory regime for such services, which is ultimately what this work seeks to do.

Important here, and further to the views of Van Niekerk regarding the attachment of importance to values, is that this is not a question of law. Instead, it is a question that when answered may dictate the choice of legal regulatory framework. In choosing such a framework, one will have to consider not only the theoretical underpinnings of the system, but the extent to which these can effectively promote the interests or values one seeks to promote. Moreover, accepting the outcome of societal order as a fundamental concern of the law, the pursuit of values through the law must also be mindful of the need for an orderly system. In this regard, as noted, the system as it stands is fragmented in terms of the unnecessary multiplication of remuneration avenues, which is anathema to any conception of an orderly system of law. For this study, in line with the contentions of Van Niekerk, this author has elected to attach more importance to the environment and its protection. With this choice, the author wishes to provide a counterapproach to the hitherto parochial focus on substantive adjustments to the law of salvage, thereby introducing an expanded canvas for value-driven development in an area of the law currently beset by inertia. This environment-first approach is ultimately the lens through which one may assess environmental services

---

26 Ibid 85.
27 See discussion in Chapters 2 and 3.

and their remuneration in the context of salvage operations, mindful of their placement in a broader pollution response matrix.

Summary of the Primary Issues Flowing from the Social Interest Theory, the Assumption of a Fundamental Ecological Norm and the Choice of Legal Regulatory Vehicles

Besides the achievement of social order as an undeniable aspect of the law, it also has utility in the realisation of values. This latter aspect may potentially differ from society to society, but it is not a question of law. In utilising the law to achieve values, mindful of the important aspect of social order, one should also strive for a system that is itself orderly. This demands that one chooses a legal regulatory vehicle to achieve specific outcomes with care, especially if one wishes to attain overall systemic coherence. In relation to societal values, the environment and its protection have become paramount and areas of the law previously unconcerned with environmental outcomes have become subject to developmental scrutiny. In this regard, the law of salvage has seen a 'greening' that appears to have reached a ceiling as far as further development is concerned. Moreover, the choice of salvage law as regulatory vehicle for the remuneration of environmental services was not premised upon a careful consideration of viable alternatives and the impact of this choice on the broader system of laws dealing with pollution response.

The next chapter will consider the historical development of salvage, which illustrates how the law of salvage, throughout its development, primarily pertained to the safeguarding of property and furthering of trade. Also, mindful of the social interest theory and the use of law as a tool in the pursuit of values or outcomes, the analysis will also show that early incarnations of salvage law in the form of provisions contained in early codes and legislation were often directed at the attainment of broader social interests. This might explain the assumption implicit in demands for changes to the law of salvage in relation to the remuneration of environmental services – that it is sufficiently adaptable to facilitate such demands.

Of course, the key problem of this assumption is precisely the fact that it is an assumption that has received no direct academic scrutiny. Moreover, the focus on the law of salvage is decidedly narrow, considering that the social environmental interest is significantly broader than the private interests that typically form the subject of discussions for change. The drivers of demands for changes to the law of salvage are also typically private interests for whom private commercial interests and the avoidance of liabilities are paramount.[28] While understandable, questions about legal

---

28 See discussion of Article 14 of the Salvage Convention in Chapter 4, p 48 ff.

development and the effective promotion of the fundamental social interest in the environment ought not to be left to the perspectives of the private industry without question.

Bibliography

Pound R, 'A Survey of Social Interests' (1943) 57 Harvard LR pp. 1–39.
Pound, R, *Social Control Through Law* (Archon Books, 1968)
Van Niekerk, 'The Ecological Norm in Law or the Jurisprudence of the Fight against Pollution' (1975) 92 SALJ 78

2 Historical Overview of Salvage

Changing Contexts and the Pursuit of Values

Academic writing on the law of salvage typically refers to the ancient origins thereof.[1] Nevertheless, while the modern legal understanding of salvage has undergone several changes,[2] including the introduction of 'special compensation' in situations where a vessel and cargo constituted a threat to the environment,[3] the safeguarding of property has been a historical constant. This was likely the result of the trade context within which this area of the law developed, and the fact that the admiralty jurisdiction, seized of salvage matters, had a distinctly property-based jurisdiction.[4] The eventual development of a liberal salvage award to encourage salvors and to further the interests of navigation and commerce was essentially the continuation of a theme established in early maritime codes, generally regarded as precursors to the modern law of salvage.[5] The other notable constant was the extent to which the law of salvage, although confined to matters of property

---

1 See Rose FD, *Kennedy and Rose on Salvage* (7th edn Thomson Reuters (Legal) Ltd, London (2010). The author describes the law of maritime salvage as an 'ancient and important part of the wider law governing marine perils and safety at sea'. At 1. See also See Clift R and Gay R, 'The Shifting Nature of Salvage Law: A View from a Distance'. (2004–05) 79 *Tul. L. Rev*, 1355.

2 Clift and Gay, 'The Shifting Nature of Salvage Law: A View from a Distance'. (2004–05) 79 *Tul. L. Rev*, 1355. The authors note the first significant change as the shift from awarding those who recovered property that had been lost to rewarding those whose efforts prevented the loss of property at sea, which was followed by the right of a vessel owner to claim an award , the emergence of professional salvors and salvage contracts, and ultimately, the introduction of 'special compensation' in situations where a vessel and cargo constituted a threat to the environment.

3 Article 14 of the 1989 Salvage Convention.

4 See Rose, 'Restitution for the Rescuer' (1989) 9 *Oxford J. Legal Stud.* 167.

5 See discussion of the Rhodian Law of the Sea and the Rolls of Oléron below.

DOI: 10.4324/9781003315506-3

and marine commerce, evidently served broader social interests beyond the private interests of the primary stakeholders consisting of salvors and property owners.

As such, this chapter serves as more than a basic chronicle of the law of salvage and the context within which it developed. It also serves to confirm the views of Pound about the functional usage of law to attain specific outcomes and to promote certain values. While this functional aspect of salvage operations and the law of salvage was primarily expressed in relation to property and commercial outcomes, it nevertheless explains current assumptions regarding the ability of this area of the law to facilitate the more recent concern with the environment in salvage operations. The relatively long history of property and commercial outcomes in salvage also provides some explanation for the evident reluctance to introduce environmental protection outcomes in a manner that might erode long-standing definitions and principles of the law of salvage.

This chapter commences with an examination of two legal codes that academic authors typically refer to when providing historical accounts of the law of salvage, namely the Rhodian Law of the Sea and the Rolls of Oléron. Not only do these codes contain provisions that may be regarded as early precursors to salvage law, but they also highlight the broader social context within which these provisions functioned and the key importance of commercial property outcomes for the law of salvage. This is followed by a discussion of the development of salvage law and its placement within the jurisdiction of the English Court of Admiralty, which impacted significantly upon the development of salvage law.[6] This development entails the development of a distinct body of salvage laws via legislation as opposed to the earlier loose-standing provisions regarding the right to a salvage award found in different Acts.[7] The discussion of the admiralty context in which the law of salvage developed again highlights the property bias of the law while also providing the necessary context to the discussion of the theoretical basis of the law of salvage in Chapter 3. This is followed by a discussion of concerns arising after the consolidation of the right to salvage, which include environmental protection concerns.

6 See below pp 23–24.
7 See below pp 25–27.

Rhodian Law of the Sea

The Rhodian Law of the Sea, as an example of an 'ancient' source of salvage law,[8] contains provisions that highlight the essential property bias of salvage while also providing good evidence of the functional value attached to the law of salvage to attain broader social interests.[9]

Part III, Chapter *XXXVIII* of the Rhodian Law provided:

> if a ship loaded with corn is caught in a gale, let the captain provide skins and the sailors work the pumps. If they are negligent and the cargo is wetted by the bilge, let the sailors pay the penalty. But if it is from the gale that the cargo is injured, let the captain and the sailors together with the merchant bear the loss; and let the captain together with the ship and the sailors receive the six-hundredths of each thing saved. If goods are to be thrown into the sea, let the merchant be the first to throw and then let the sailors take a hand. Moreover, none of the sailors is to steal. If any one (*sic*) steals, let the robber make it good twofold and lose his whole gain.[10]

Chapter *XL* provided that where

> [a] ship is wrecked, and part of the cargo and the ship is saved. The passengers have on them gold or silver or whole silks or pearls. Let the gold that is saved proved a tenth, and the silver contribute a fifth. Let the whole silks, if they are saved dry, contribute a tenth, as being equal to gold. If they are wetted, let an allowance be made for the abrasion and the wetting, and let them come into contribution on that footing. Let the pearls according to their valuation contribute to the loss like a cargo of gold.[11]

These provisions were evidently concerned with the regulation of situations consequential to shipwreck. As such, they were directed at specific

---

8 Clift R and Gay R, 79 *Tul. L. Rev* (n 2), 1355. The authors note that it is 'conventional to begin discussions of the law of salvage with references to maritime codes of great antiquity, including the Laws of the Rhodians, … and the Laws of Oléron'. At 1357.

9 For the purpose of this study, for an appropriate English translation of the Rhodian Sea Law, the seminal work of Ashburner W, *The Rhodian Sea-Law Edited from the Manuscripts* (The Clarendon Press, Oxford, 1909), has been used as primary reference.

10 Ibid 112.

11 Ibid 114.

mischiefs. While the first provision spells out the rights and duties of the captain and sailors of a ship 'caught in a gale', the second relates primarily to the question of contributions to be made by merchants and passengers where goods are saved following a shipwreck. Nevertheless, the idea of a reward to those that rescue property, although restricted to those on board the ship, was established. The specific mention of 'a ship loaded with corn' suggests a limited sphere of application for the provision, namely the ills pertaining to the transportation of goods.

The criminal penalty attached to the first provision also provides insight into the regard the drafters had for the sailors on board such ships. Nevertheless, at the centre of the mischief addressed was the notion of the safeguarding of property involved in the maritime adventure. Ashburner, in commenting on the possible reasoning behind the above provisions, noted that 'that there was no hard and fast line between the mariner and the pirate' and that the object of these provisions was 'to offer a counterpoise to the temptations of a large booty'.[12]

Thus, the purpose of the reward payable to the captain and sailors, as an early kernel of salvage, had more to do with the encouragement of proper behaviour on the part of those involved in the adventure as well as their exertions in saving property. The prevailing dangers of the time provided the context for these provisions and the likelihood of piracy, and the possibility of shipwreck featured prominently. These provisions, informed by the social realities and aims of their time, evidently expressed the prevalent values at the time[13] and provide good evidence of the functional usage of law in the attainment of specific outcomes. This same phenomenon of laws drafted to address specific concerns can also be noted in later codes although the central concern with the safeguarding of property remained.

---

12 Ibid cclxii. See also Sanborn F, Origins *of the Early English Maritime and Commercial Law* (The Century Co, New York London, 1930) 37–39.
13 For a brief reference to some of the unsavoury elements of life at sea, see Runyan TJ 'The Rolls of Oléron and the Admiralty Court in Fourteenth Century England' (1975) 19(2) *The American Journal of Legal History* 95. The author notes that 'life at sea was harsh, and those who chose it and persevered were up to the challenge. They acted as individuals at sea and behaved only as well as forced to under the command of their masters. The tales of keelhauling, drownings (*sic*) and piratical massacres leave the impression of lawless men on a lawless sea'. At 95.

Rolls of Oléron

The Rolls of Oléron have been described as '[t]he most influential to emerge in northern Europe during the Middle Ages'.[14] This code has been traced back to the judgments of the Maritime Court of the island of Oléron, a port city in the province of Bordeaux.[15] The 'burgeoning wine trade' between England, Aquitaine, and Flanders appears to be the context within which the Rolls were adopted.[16] The Rolls have also influenced the development of English law.[17] In this regard, Holdsworth noted that

> England based its maritime law upon the laws of Oléron just as the other sea-port towns which bordered upon the Mediterranean, the Atlantic Ocean, the English Channel, or the North Sea based their law upon similar codes of maritime usage.[18]

Frankot also refers to 'a mention of the laws in a report written in the 12th year of Edward III's reign (1329) [which] confirms that the laws were in use in England in the first half of the 14th century'.[19] As an expression of the

---

14 Cumming CS, 'The English High Court of Admiralty' (1993) 17 *Tul. Mar. L.J.* 209, 214–215. See also Paulsen GW, 'An Historical Overview of the Development of Uniformity in International Maritime Law' (1983) 57 *Tul. L. Rev.* 1065, 1067.

15 Ibid. Cumming, 215 and Paulsen, 1070.

16 Hutton N, 'The Origin, Development and Future of Maritime Liens and the Action in Rem' (2003) 28 *Tul. Mar. L.J.* 81. See also Cumming (n 14) 215.

17 See Rose FD (n 4) 3. See also, Sanborn (n 12). *The English Black Book of Admiralty*, which is a compilation of official documents copied by the English Exchequer of the Middle Ages, contains as the 4th document a copy of the Rolls of Oléron. However, the original 24 articles of the Rolls have been expanded by an additional 18 articles. See Mangone G, 'Commerce by Water: All Cases of Admiralty and Maritime Jurisdiction' (1993) 11 *Del. Law*. Also see Holdsworth WS, *A History of English Law* (1903, Volumes *I* to *III*) (1924, Volumes *IV* and *V*) Methuen & Co, London. Paulsen GW (n14) at 1070, expresses uncertainty on whether these laws were stated by Eleanor, the mother of England's Kind Richard I or by the King himself while in Oléron on his return from the Crusades. Nevertheless, he contends that this code became accepted as maritime law in both England and France after Richard I inherited Oléron on the death of his mother.

18 Holdsworth WS, *A History of English Law* vol *V* (1924) 129. For an account of how the Rolls of Oléron might have become relevant in England see Hutton N (n 16), 81.

19 Frankot E, 'Medieval Maritime Law from Oléron to Wisby: Jurisdictions in the Law of the Sea' in Communities in Montojo JP and Pedersen F (eds) *European History: Representations, Jurisdictions, Conflicts Representations Jurisdictions Conflicts* (Edizioni Plus Pisa University Press Pisa 2007) 151–172, 153.
    This report claims that Richard I (1189–99) wrote the laws at Oléron on his way back from the Holy Land and subsequently brought them to England.

values and norms of its times, the Rolls of Oléron and those provisions that relate to salvage mirror the earlier Rhodian Sea laws.[20]

Article iii provided that

> [i]f any vessel, through misfortune, happens to be cast away, in what-soever place it be, the mariners shall be obliged to use their best endeavours for saving as much of the ship and lading as possibly they can; and if they preserve part thereof, the master shall allow them a reasonable consideration to carry them home to their own country. And in case they save enough to enable the master to do this, he may lawfully pledge to some honest persons such part thereof as may by sufficient for that occasion. But if they have not endeavoured to save as aforesaid then the master shall not be bound to provide for them in any thing (sic), but ought to keep them in safe custody, until he know the pleasure of the owners, in which he may act as becomes a prudent master; for if he does otherwise, he shall be obliged to make satisfaction.

In a similar vein to the above passage, Article iv provided:

> If a vessel ... happens in the course of her voyage, to be rendered unfit to proceed therein, and the mariners save as much of the lading as pos-sibly they can; if the merchants require their goods of the master, he may deliver them if he pleases, they paying the freight in proportion to the part of the voyage that is performed, and the costs of the salvage. But if the master can readily repair his vessel, he may do it; or if he pleases, he may freight another ship to perform his voyage. And if he has promised the people who helped him to save the ship the third, or the half part of the goods saved for the danger they ran, the judicatures of the country should consider the pains and trouble they have been at, without any regard to the promises made them by the parties concerned in the time of their distress.

Article iii concerns the duties of mariners in the event of a maritime misfortune and their entitlements upon their fulfilling these duties. The direction to the master to allow them reasonable consideration upon the

---

20 It is evident from a reading of the Rolls of Oléron that, while perhaps better developed, it has taken over some of the provisions of the Rhodian Sea law. See Sanborn F (n 12) 37. In terms of provisions relating to salvage, it appears as if similar concerns informed the draft-ing of the provisions of the Rolls of Oléron as the Rhodian Sea Law.

performance of their duties appears to be in consideration of these duties. It is also likely that this consideration would have encouraged mariners to perform their duties. Article iv, in spelling out the options available to the shipmaster *vis à vis* the merchants in the event of a vessel being unfit to proceed on her voyage and where the mariners have saved the lading, would have a similar outcome in mind. Like the provisions in the Rhodian Sea laws, the purpose and aims of the rules involved the prevention of ills perceived as consequential upon shipwreck and, implicitly, the safeguarding of property.

In the context of trade at sea and the prevalent ills concomitant therewith, the functional value of the provisions can be appreciated. Aside from the obvious intricacies of this trade, these rules were clearly drafted against the backdrop of what were major concerns of the time. These concerns related primarily to navigational dangers due to 'the violence of weather',[21] and those, both on land and at sea, that sought to capitalise upon the misfortunes intrinsic to sea trade.

While academic writers[22] tend to refer to these early codes when commenting on the origins of salvage, circumstances were clearly different and provisions relating to salvage were narrow in operation and directed at specific mischiefs. Moreover, the purpose was not so much the encouragement of volunteers as the furthering of trade and the prevention of specific ills. Essentially, the interests of commerce and trade were furthered by encouraging or discouraging certain types of behaviour to safeguard property. The theme of safeguarding of property was therefore established early in the development of the law of salvage and one can observe how it was of fundamental importance in a broader trade context. From a social interest theory perspective, matters were relatively simple, and priorities were relatively clear as there were no obvious other broader social interests, such as protection of the environment, to be balanced against marine commerce and trade outcomes.

---

21 Article XXIX of the Rolls of Oléron makes express reference to the 'violence of the weather' and the actions of 'the lord of [a] place or country, where ... misfortune ... happen' that 'ought to be aiding and assisting ... in saving ... shipwrecked goods, and ... without the least embezzlement, or taking any part thereof from the right owners'.

22 Ashburner W, *The Rhodian Sea-Law edited from the manuscripts* (The Clarendon Press, Oxford, 1909), Sanborn, *Origins of the Early English Maritime and Commercial Law* (The Century Co, New York London, 1930), Clift R and Gay R, 'The Shifting Nature of Salvage Law: A View from a Distance'. (2004–05) 79 *Tul. L. Rev*, 1355, Staniland H, '*Shipping*' in Joubert, WA and Faris, J (eds), *LAWSA Vol. 25(2) reissue 1* (Butterworths 2006).

Early English Admiralty Jurisdiction and Salvage

The basic principles of salvage law in England were laid down by decisions of the Admiralty Court.[23] Moreover, much of the development of early English salvage law was closely linked the development of the English Court of Admiralty, and two important aspects of Admiralty jurisdiction. The first was that the Admiralty Court functioned as a court of Equity, which means that it was not bound by *stare decisis*.[24] In this regard, Lord Stowell noted the extent to which the technical rigidity of the common law sometimes failed to 'reach the real justice of a case'.[25] However, the Admiralty Court as 'a Court of Equity .... [had to] determine the cases submitted to its cognizance upon equitable principles, and according to the rules of natural justice'.[26] Essentially, this allowed the court to devise appropriate remedies such as an award for the rescue of property (salvage), thereby escaping the confines of the common law. Therefore, the court could achieve results that were just in the circumstances before it.

This explains notions such as that advanced by Holdsworth that, 'no technical jurisprudence peculiar to any country would have been satisfactory to traders coming from many different countries'.[27] In this regard, the Admiralty Court's equitable approach to disputes between traders made all the more sense as merchants would have preferred rules that they were more familiar with,[28] and that were not steeped in the peculiarities or technicalities of a foreign system of law. This aspect of the Admiralty Court's jurisdiction also explains the extent to which earlier codes, such as the Rolls of Oléron found application via the Admiralty Court. In this regard, Holdsworth noted that the collection of customs recorded in the Black Book of Admiralty,[29] which included the Rolls of Oléron, was distinct from anything at common law and 'of the contents of this customary law the common law courts ... knew very little'.[30] To the extent that early codes such as the Rolls were included in the Black Book of Admiralty, one would have been able to pre-empt the assumption of jurisdiction by the Admiralty Court over commercial matters and, of course, shipwreck and salvage, the latter which was

23 Rose FD (n 1) 1.
24 The Juliana (1822) 2 Dods. 504.
25 Ibid. At 520.
26 Ibid.
27 Holdsworth W (n 17) 543.
28 Holdsworth WA (n 17). The author notes that 'the civil law procedure of the Admiralty, because it was based on the technical ideas of the civil law, was far more intelligible to the foreign merchant than the procedure of the common law courts'. At 128.
29 Ibid.
30 Ibid.

expressly included in 19th-century legislation (the 1840 and 1861 Victorian Acts)[31] as a head of Admiralty jurisdiction.[32]

The second important aspect of the Admiralty Court's jurisdiction, which impacted on the law of salvage, was the fact that it was a property-based jurisdiction.[33] In this regard, early Admiralty jurisdiction in matters pertaining to salvage were largely a matter of property that had become wreck.[34] In this regard, it has been noted that 'what may be called the land jurisdiction, as opposed to the Admiralty jurisdiction, was concerned with wreck alone, and the Admiralty jurisdiction was concerned mainly, if not entirely, with flotsam, jetsam, lagan, and derelict'.[35] In this sense, the modern idea of preventing shipwreck was absent. Moreover, some early statutes pertaining to salvage had less to do with the rights of the rescuer of property to an award, than the retention of title by the original owner. Thus, a statute of 1275 provided that

> [c]oncerning Wrecks of the Sea, it is agreed, that where a Man, a Dog, or a Cat escape quick out of the Ship, that such Ship nor Barge, nor any Thing within them, shall be adjudged Wreck: (2) but the Goods shall be saved and kept by View of the Sheriff, Coroner, or the King's Bailiff, *and* the Hands of such as are of the Town where the Goods were found; (3) so that if any sue for those Goods, and after prove that they were *his or perished* in his Keeping, within a Year and a Day, they shall be restored to him without Delay; and if not, they shall remain to the King.[36]

Thus, any shipwrecked goods would be restored to an owner who could prove title, while unclaimed wreck would belong to the Crown.[37] Title passing to the crown, of course, had bestowed considerable benefits upon the Admiral as the rights of the Crown to unclaimed wreck on the high seas were granted to the Admiral, thus becoming perquisites of the Admiral.[38] This suggests that the extension of Admiralty jurisdiction and the eventual jurisdictional jostling between the Admiralty and common

---

31 The Victorian statutes, regulating jurisdiction and practice in admiralty. 3 & 4 Vict. C65 (1840); 9 & 10 Vict c 99.
32 Victorian Act of 1840 s 6.
33 Rose FD (1989) 9 *Oxford J. Legal Stud.* (n 4) 167.
34 Ibid. 64.
35 Ibid. 66.
36 The Statute of Westminster I (1275). 3 Edw. 1 c 4.
37 Ibid.
38 Rose FD (n 1) 65.

law courts cannot be divorced entirely from extra-legal socio-political and economic factors.[39] Nevertheless, like the provisions relating to salvage in earlier codes such as the Rolls of Oléron, legislative efforts were functional, directed at specific outcomes and expressive of a particular value background.

While it is unclear when the modern notion of the prevention of disaster was accepted as a salvage service worthy of reward,[40] the primary means of establishing the right to a reward was by statute. The informing rationale for these legislative developments was the concern for the safeguarding of ships and goods on board such ships. In this regard, Rose[41] refers to an Act of 1713,[42] which was aimed at the protection of ships and their owners by providing for rewards for salvage services rendered on or near the coast. While the purpose of the Act was the prevention of the stranding of ships, it was unlike modern salvage in that those who would render such assistance would have been ordered (i.e., their actions were not voluntary as required in the law of salvage) by a sheriff, justice of the peace, customs officers or other public officers.[43] The apparent failure of this Act to successfully achieve the aims behind its enactment led to further legislation.[44]

The preamble to Act 26 Geo. II, c. 19 of 1753 specifically refers to prior legislation and 'the many wicked enormities [that] had been committed' and 'grievous Damage of Merchants and Mariners of our own and other Countries'. Various penalties are then provided where those lawfully authorised by the Act

> shall be assaulted, beaten and wounded, for or on account of the exercise of his or their duty, in or concerning the salvage or preservation of

---

39 Hofmeyer G, 'Admiralty Jurisdiction in South Africa' (1982) *Acta Juridica* 30. The author, commenting on the development of the law and admiralty notes that '[i]t was shaped by the exigencies of maritime commerce, suppressed in England by the jealousy of the courts of common law (a jealousy which was fanned by parochialism, financial self-interest and antipathy towards the civil law) and given impetus by the chance events of history'. At 30. See also Melikan R, 'Shippers, salvors, and sovereigns: Competing interests in the mediaeval law of Shipwreck' (1990) *The Journal of Legal History* 11.2 163. The author describes the law of shipwreck in mediaeval England as feudal, which implies a particular value system as underlying the law. In the modern era, it would of course be the value attached to environmental protection that informs current attempts at changing the law of salvage.
40 Rose FD (n 1) 65.
41 Ibid 67.
42 12 Anne c. 18 (1713).
43 Rose (n 1) 67.
44 Ibid.

any ship or vessel in distress, or of any ship or vessel, goods or effects, stranded, wrecked, or cast on shore, or lying under water, in any of his majesty's dominions.[45]

Thus, with the appropriate penalties in place, the Act not only punished those that might have exploited or caused incidents of shipwreck, but also encouraged those that prevented disasters. It went further than the earlier 1713 Act by also providing for a reward for those that may not have been instructed by the appropriate official to render services:

> In case any person or persons not employed by the master, mariners or owners, or other persons lawfully authorized, in the salvage of any ship or vessel, or the cargo or provision thereof, shall, in the absence of persons so employed or authorized save any such ship, vessel, goods or effects, and cause the same to be carried, for the benefit of the owners or proprietors, into port, or to any near adjoining custom house or other place of safe custody, ... be entitled to a reasonable reward ... in like manner as the salvage is to be adjusted and paid by virtue of the statute made in the twelfth year of the reign of her late Majesty Queen Anne.[46]

The reference to the Act of Queen Anne in the above extract would be the 1713 Act,[47] which originally introduced the notion of services to prevent shipwreck. The Act, however, goes further by mentioning an issue pertinent to the modern concept of salvage, namely, the volunteer salvor being entitled to a reward.[48] However, considering the title to the Act, Stealing Shipwrecked Goods Act 1753, the introduction of this concept, part and parcel of the modern concept of salvage, was evidently part of the response to other social realities of the times. In this sense, the above Acts, just like those enacted subsequently, often addressed very particular concerns that included salvage-related matters but were not necessarily restricted thereto. This appears to be mirrored in the current way in which salvage operations appear to fit a broader environmental protection framework. The key difference, however, is that the broader context to the salvage aspects of the 1753 Act is still a property protection context

---

45   26 Geo. II c 19 s *XI*.
46   Ibid s *V*.
47   See above n 42.
48   See above n 46.

and of direct relevance to the actions of salvors in performing salvage operations.

The Acts of 1809,[49] 1813,[50] and 1821[51] are further examples of legislation that have incrementally added to a growing body of salvage law. The Act of 1809 is expressly directed at the 'preventing of frauds and depredations committed on merchants, ship owners, and underwriters, by boatmen and others; and also for remedying certain defects relative to the adjustment of salvage in England under an act made in the twelfth year of Queen Anne'.[52] The Act not only remedies the perceived defects of the earlier 1713 Act[53] but also extends its application to those of its provisions dealing with the salvage, sale, and marking of anchors.[54]

The later 1813 Act,[55] in addition to conferring concurrent jurisdiction on the Admiralty and common law courts, provided for the rights of carriages to pass over land in order to reach vessels and goods for the purpose of salvage services. Nevertheless, all these legislative developments were directed at specific aims addressed via provisions found in different Acts and all involved property. This piecemeal approach to matters relating to salvage changed with the enactment of the English Wreck and Salvage Act, 1846. Rose notes that 'the rights to salvage separately conferred by various previous Acts were consolidated'.[56] In this sense, more than a hundred years before the incorporation of the 1989 Salvage Convention into English law, salvage became a subject of statutory regulation in its own right and singularly concerned with the safeguarding of property. More importantly, this safeguarding of property was directly related to the broader interest in the furtherance of marine commerce and trade. This explains the limited property reach of definitions developed in salvage[57] and the obvious challenges this may present in the pursuit of environmental outcomes.

---

49 49 Geo. III, c. 122.

50 Frauds by Boatmen Act, 53 Geo. III, c 87.

51 Frauds by Boatmen Act Acts 1 & 2 Geo. IV, c. 75.

52 This is the long title of the 1809 Act. For Act in the 12th year of Queen Anne, see above n 42.

53 12 Anne c. 18 (1713). See above n 42.

54 See Rose FD (n 1) 68.

55 See above n 50.

56 Rose FD (n 1) 70.

57 See discussion in Chapters 3 and 4.

Further Changes Following the Consolidation of the Right to Claim Salvage and New Environmental Protection Concerns

Technological advancements also impacted upon developments in salvage and salvage law. In this regard, one may note the invention of the steam tug as a direct cause for the development of a corps of professional salvors, which triggered further developments in the law[58] and changed the basis of salvage compensation.[59] In *The Glengyle*,[60] the House of Lords, *per* Lord Shand, attached

> a very great importance to the circumstances that these ships [salvage steamers] had crews specially fitted for the service, that they had captains who were apparently familiar with several languages in order that they might perform their services thoroughly, and that they had appliances which were suited for saving vessels in distress. All those are considerations which ought to weigh with the court in assessing the amount which ought to be given by way of salvage.

The notion of a liberal salvage award was used to encourage the professional salvor to maintain the necessary equipment for salvage services. In this regard, in elucidating the encouragement element of salvage awards, the Court of Appeal in *The Glengyle*[61] also referred with approval to an earlier judgment of Lord Stowell:[62]

> The principles upon which the Court of Admiralty proceeds lead to a liberal remuneration in salvage cases, for they look not merely to the exact quantum of service performed in the case itself, but to the general interests of navigation and commerce of the country, which are greatly protected by exertions of this nature.

---

58 The performance of salvage services was less personal in that the chief instrument of salvage was the salving vessel rather than the physical exertions of the crew. Also see Clift R and Gay R (above n 22), 1355, 1361. It is almost to be expected that business-minded individuals would seize upon the opportunities provided by powered vessels to provide a service that is highly lucrative.

59 Clift R and Gay (n 22), 1355, 1361.

60 [1898] A.C. 519 (H.L). 8 Asp Mar Law Cas 436.

61 8 Asp Mar Law Cas. 341.

62 *The William Beckford* 3 C. Rob. 355.

From the above it is again evident that the development of the law, being concerned with private property interests, was ultimately in service to 'the general interests of navigation and commerce of the country'. Therefore, a close relationship between technological development, the birth of the professional salvor and the extent to which the law can be used to pursue practical benefits is apparent. Also, a liberal salvage award is used to further the interests of navigation and commerce, which is not at all different from the way earlier loose-standing salvage provisions functioned.

The birth of the professional salvor[63] also led to salvage services performed under contract, which gradually replaced the general maritime law of salvage. In this regard, the standard form Lloyd's Form of Salvage Agreement (LOF) has become the most widely used contract under which salvage services are rendered. Changes to the standard form (devised towards the end of the 1800s) were made from time to time 'to accommodate developments in case law, practice, and technological and other changes'.[64] It was also LOF, although much later, that provided us with the first attempts, albeit by the contracting parties themselves, to recognise an environmental dimension to the provision of salvage services by creating a financial incentive for salvors to become involved in rescue operations that could prevent pollution.[65]

Regarding the 'greening of salvage law', marine disasters such as those involving the *Torrey Canyon (*1967) and the *Amoco Cadiz (*1978) drove home the impacts of maritime casualties on the marine environment.[66] These incidents also highlighted the utility value of salvors and their unique expertise in dealing with such matters. Therefore, given the central involvement of salvors, it comes as no surprise that changes to the legal framework regulating salvors and salvage operations would be considered. Attempts to align salvage operations with environmental protection aims became the order of the day. While the original efforts were in the form of contractual

---

63 Rose FD (n 1), 72 and 400.

64 Ibid 401.

65 For a detailed discussion of salvage contracts and the promotion of the public interest in environmental protection, see Cupido DM, 'The Environment in Shipping Incidents: Salvage Contracts and the Public Interest' in Osuji, Ngwu, Dima Jamali (eds), *Corporate Social Responsibility in Developing and Emerging Markets* (CUP 2019) pp 206–231.

66 Redgwell C, 'The greening of Salvage Law' (1990)14 *Marine Policy* 142, 142, fn 3; Gold E, 'Marine Salvage: Towards a New Regime' (1989) 20 *Journal of Maritime Law and Commerce* 487, 489; Kerr M, 'The International Convention on Salvage 1989 – How It Came to Be' (1990) 39 *International and Comparative Law Quarterly* 530, 535. The Liberian tanker, *Amoco Cadiz*, came into distress as a result of a steering failure and the ship and her cargo were finally lost off the coast of Brittany and could not be salvaged.

provisions such as in Lloyd's Open Form (LOF 1980), these were followed by the Montreal Draft Salvage Convention of 1981 and ultimately the International Salvage Convention of 1989.[67] The 1989 Salvage Convention is generally regarded as a direct consequence of the 1978 *Amoco Cadiz* disaster, which saw 1 300 000 tons of oil being released into the ocean off the French Atlantic coast.[68] In this regard, Redgwell has noted that the *Amoco Cadiz* disaster was a 'useful starting point for a discussion of the greening of salvage law',[69] a process that culminated in and was supposed to be reflected in the 1989 Salvage Convention.

Concluding Remarks

This chapter, in providing a historical overview of the law of salvage, highlighted the functional value of this system of law to address broader social concerns and to respond to new challenges. However, much of the development of the law of salvage took place in response to commercial and property outcomes and, in the English context, in a court with a property-based jurisdiction. Nevertheless, the central involvement of salvors in operations where there was the threat of environmental damage might explain assumptions that the law of salvage, which regulate their activities, could be shaped to address the demand for environmental outcomes. The key challenge is that environmental outcomes, unlike preceding challenges in the early maritime codes and later legislative efforts, had no obvious relationship with the safeguarding of private property. Nevertheless, an already existing framework of salvage law regulating operations, as happened with the Salvage Convention, would necessarily be in the spotlight for changes to address this new concern. Even more so, if the discussion of changes to the law is driven from the perspective of the traditional actors in salvage operations. However, from an environmentalist perspective and a view of environmental protection as a fundamental concern, it remains to be seen whether the law of salvage can effectively facilitate this additional concern. More so, given the extent to which environmental protection services differ from one constant featured throughout history, namely, the safeguarding of property to promote the broader interest in the furthering of marine commerce. This, as will be shown in the next two chapters, shaped the common

---

67 FD FD (n 1).

68 Ibid 208.

69 Redgwell C (n 66) 142. The author notes that the disaster was the 'impetus for a number of changes in the international law of salvage'.

law of salvage in a way that would always present difficulties for the effective pursuit of environmental protection outcomes via mechanisms devised
in the law of salvage.

Bibliography

Ashburner W, *The Rhodian Sea-Law Edited from the Manuscripts* (The Clarendon
    Press, 1909)

Clift R and Gay R, 'The Shifting Nature of Salvage Law: A View from a Distance'
    (2004–2005) 79 Tul. L. Rev 1355

Cumming CS, 'The English High Court of Admiralty' (1993) 17 Tul. Mar. L.J. 209,
    214–215

Cupido DM, 'The Environment in Shipping Incidents: Salvage Contracts and the
    Public Interest' in N Osuji and D Jamali (eds), *Corporate Social Responsibility
    in Developing and Emerging Markets* (CUP 2019), pp. 206–231

Frankot E, 'Medieval Maritime Law from Oléron to Wisby: Jurisdictions in the
    Law of the Sea' in Communities in JP Montojo and F Pedersen (eds), *European
    History: Representations, Jurisdictions, Conflicts Representations Jurisdictions
    Conflicts* (Edizioni Plus Pisa University Press Pisa 2007) pp. 151–172.

Hofmeyer G, 'Admiralty Jurisdiction in South Africa' (1982) 1982 Acta Juridica 30

Holdsworth WS, *A History of English Law* (Methuen & Co. Ltd 1903, Volumes I to
    III) (1924, Volumes IV and V)

Hutton N, 'The Origin, Development and Future of Maritime Liens and the Action
    in Rem' (2003) 28 Tul. Mar. L.J. 81

Kerr M, 'The International Convention on Salvage 1989 – How it came to be' (1990)
    39 International and Comparative Law Quarterly 530, 535

Mangone G, 'Commerce by Water: All Cases of Admiralty and Maritime Jurisdiction'
    (1993) 11 Del. Law 28–43

Melikan R, 'Shippers, Salvors, and Sovereigns: Competing Interests in the
    Mediaeval Law of Shipwreck' (1990) 11(2) The Journal of Legal History 163

Paulsen GW, 'An Historical Overview of the Development of Uniformity in
    International Maritime Law' (1983) 57 Tul. L. Rev. 1065, 1067

Redgwell C, 'The greening of Salvage Law' (1990) 14 Marine Policy 142, fn 3;
    Edgar Gold 'Marine Salvage: Towards a New Regime' (1989) 20 Journal of
    Maritime Law and Commerce 487, 489

Rose FD, 'Restitution for the Rescuer' (1989) 9 Oxford J. Legal Stud. 167

Rose FD, *Kennedy and Rose on Salvage* (7th edn, Thomson Reuters (Legal) Limited
    2010)

Runyan TJ, 'The Rolls of Oléron and the Admiralty Court in Fourteenth Century
    England' (1975) 19(2) The American Journal of Legal History 95

Sanborn F, *Origins of the Early English Maritime and Commercial Law* (The
    Century Co. 1930)

Staniland H, 'Shipping' in WA Joubert and J Faris (eds), *LAWSA Vol. 25(2) reissue
    1* (Butterworths 2006)

3 Theory of Salvage and Environmental Protection

This chapter examines the theoretical basis and nature of the law of salvage and the extent to which it could be aligned with environmental protection concerns. In this regard, it should be noticed that, while the law of salvage is regulated at supra-national level in the form of the International Salvage Convention, the instrument does not tell us about the theoretical underpinnings of this area of the law. As such, this is a question for which one must refer to the common law. An examination of the legal theoretical basis of the right to salvage will allow for a more complete understanding of potential linkages between the law of salvage and environmental protection outcomes. In this regard, this chapter ultimately demonstrates that the theoretical underpinnings of the law of salvage, which developed in a restricted property-based admiralty context, do not lend itself to environmental outcomes in a manner that elevates this broader social interest relative to commercial and property outcomes.

The chapter commences with a discussion of the basic academic definitions of salvage. This is followed by an analysis of the legal nature and theoretical underpinnings of salvage law to determine how these may or may not link salvage law with environmental protection outcomes.

Definition of Salvage

A good starting point for an understanding of the reach of salvage would be to provide a working definition. In this regard, Lord Stowell observed:

> no exact definition of salvage is given in any of the books. I do not know that it has, and I should be sorry to limit it by any definition now.[1]

---

1 *The Governor Raffles* (1815) 2 Dods. 14, 17.

DOI: 10.4324/9781003315506-4

Nevertheless, while a definition may not necessarily capture the totality of this area of law, it may help with the identification of its salient attributes or concerns. Academic scholars have provided basic definitions of salvage, typically with reference to the underlying elements of a successful salvage claim. Rose, despite acknowledging the limitations of legal definitions, has provided the following as a working definition of salvage:

> [A] service which confers a benefit by saving or helping to save a recognised subject of salvage when in danger from which it cannot be extricated unaided, if and so far as the rendering of such service is voluntary in the sense of being attributable neither to a pre-existing obligation, nor solely for the interests of the salvor.[2]

Brice, although worded differently, provides a definition of salvage that includes the same basic elements.[3]

> In English law a right to salvage arises when a person, acting as a volunteer (that is without any pre-existing contractual or other legal duty so to act) preserves or contributes to preserving at sea any vessel, cargo, freight or other recognised subject of salvage from danger.[4]

From these two academic definitions, one can distil the basic legal elements of salvage operations. The service must be voluntary, and it must be successfully performed to a recognisable subject of salvage in peril. Rose expands the elements somewhat further by noting that salvage applies where:

> (i) In maritime circumstances (ii) there is a recognised subject of salvage (iii) which has come into a position of danger necessitating a salvage service to preserve it from loss or damage and (iv) a person falling within the classification of salvors (traditionally called a volunteer) (v) is successful or meritoriously contributes to success in preserving the subject from danger.[5]

Both of the definitions provided by Rose and Brice confirm that salvage law is concerned primarily with the saving or preservation of property in peril

---

2 Rose FD, *Kennedy and Rose on Salvage* (7th edn Thomson *Reuters* (Legal) Limited, London (2010)) 8.
3 Reeder, *Brice on Maritime Salvage* (4th edn, Sweet & Maxwell, 2003).
4 Ibid 1.
5 Rose FD (n 2).

at sea or the saving or preservation of property in maritime circumstances.[6] This limitation, as noted in the preceding chapter, is likely the result of the admiralty context in which salvage developed, which was a property-based jurisdiction.[7] This would necessarily have influenced the formulation of the elements of salvage contained in the definitions provided.

Nothing in the above definitions, expressly or implicitly, links the law of salvage to environmental protection, given that they expressly define the services performed by salvors as a service to property.[8] Also, services to the marine and coastal environment are not by any stretch of the imagination services to 'a vessel or property in navigable waters' as required by these definitions. In this regard, Lord Stowell's hesitance to provide a definition of salvage law proved to be well founded as it is unlikely that any definition attempted in the year 1815 would have been mindful of future environmental protection demands. The current value attached to the environment is a relatively recent development, and environmental concerns would not have been a factor in the formulation of definitions at the time.

It is also unlikely that a court would have been able to simply introduce the environment as either a subject or outcome of salvage operations without falling afoul of the notion that judges do not make law. In this regard, in *The Nagasaki Spirit*,[9] Lord Mustill, noting the 'widespread contamination of sea, foreshore and wildlife' resulting from the escape of cargo from the wreck of the *Torrey Canyon*, observed that

> the traditional law of salvage provided no answer, for the only success which mattered was success in preserving the ship, cargo and associated interests; and this was logical, since the owners of those interests, who had to bear any salvage award that was made, had no financial stake in the protection of anything else.[10]

The environment and concerns about its protection were simply not an issue in earlier years. Definitions formulated at the time would, necessarily, have limited the scope of an area of the law that, in modern times, is closely asso-ciated with environmental protection. This judicial conservatism of Lord

---

6 Brice on Salvage above (n 3) 397. Also see Rose FD (n 2) 1.

7 See Rose FD, 'Restitution for the Rescuer' (1989) 9 *Oxford J. Legal Stud.* 167.

8 See Rose FD, Kennedy and Rose on Salvage (n 2). Professor Rose notes that the traditional law of salvage was inadequate to provide a resolution of environmental issues which would satisfy the interests of all the parties involved when a casualty arises. At 207. Also see Shaw R, 'The 1989 Salvage Convention and English Law' (1989) *L.M.C.L.Q* 202.

9 *Semco Salvage & Marine Pte Ltd v Lancer Navigation Co Ltd (The Nagasaki Spirit)* [1997] 1 Lloyd's Rep. 323 [HL].

10 Ibid 327.

Mustill appears to be driven by a decidedly rule-based approach as opposed to a results-driven approach as called for by Pound's social interest theory and any acknowledgement of environmental protection as a fundamental norm. The key take from Lord Mustill's approach is that the rules of salvage were too rigid to allow for the kind of environmental activism called for by an approach that posits environmental protection as a fundamental concern. The rules simply did not allow for the kind of judicial creativity one might have to employ should one wish to account for a broader interest in environmental protection. Here one may add that an attempt to include environmental services in the definition of salvage would essentially amount to a change that fundamentally alters the identity of this area of the law.

Lord Mustill, in contrast with Pound's social interest theory, focussed on the individual interests of those involved in salvage operations rather than any broader social interests. Nevertheless, it is likely that a more conscious consideration of the broader social interest in environmental protection would have resulted in the same outcome, as doing more would have amounted to a case of judicial overreaching in the face of clear legal definitions. As such, any attempt to expand upon these definitions will have to emanate from legislative efforts.[11]

The Equitable Nature of Salvage

In English law, salvage is regarded as being of an equitable nature,[12] which essentially allowed it to depart from the common law principle that unrequested benefits are typically not permissible.[13] In this regard, In *Falcke v Scottish Imperial Insurance Co*,[14] it was held that

> work and labour done, or money expended by one man to preserve or benefit the property of another do not according to English law create a lien upon the property saved or benefited, nor, even if standing alone, create any obligation to repay the expenditure. Liabilities are not to be forced on people behind their backs any more than you can confer a benefit upon a man against his will.[15]

---

11 See discussion of the Salvage Convention in Chapter 4, 42 *ff*.
12 In *The Goring* [1987]2 All ER 246, Sir Donaldson MR, notes that 'salvage law is based ...
   [on] equity [and] public policy. At 252. See also Rose FD (n 2) 11.
13 *Falcke v Scottish Imperial Insurance Co* (1886) 34 CH.D 234.
14 Ibid.
15 Ibid 248–249.

In contradistinction to the common law principle, salvage afforded the salvor a right to a reward. In this regard, Sir Christopher Robin, in *The Calypso*,[16] noted that:

> Salvage resolves ... [itself] into the equity of rewarding spontaneous services rendered in the protection of the lives and property of others. This is a general principle of natural equity: and it was considered as giving a cause of action in the Roman law; and from that source it was adopted by jurisdictions of this nature in the different countries of Europe.[17]

The above description not only represents a significant departure from the Common Law principle but also recognises the continental roots of the system, with its reference to salvage rewarding spontaneous services as a general principle of natural equity under Roman law. Rose, in expanding upon and explaining this general equitable base of salvage, suggests that it is founded upon two considerations, namely the public policy of encouragement and the benefits conferred by salvors.[18]

Public Policy

In relation to the public policy of encouragement, Dr Lushington, in *The Fusilier*, remarked that

> [s]alvage is not governed by the ordinary rules which prevail in mercantile transactions on shore. Salvage is governed by a due regard to benefit received, combined with a just regard for the general interests of ships and marine commerce. All owners of ships and cargoes and all underwriters are interested in the great principle of adequate remuneration being paid for salvage services; and none are more interested than the underwriters of the cargo.[19]

Clear from the remarks of Dr Lushington is that, aside from the benefits conferred,[20] salvage is aimed at broader policy considerations such as the general interests of ships and marine commerce. This broader interest

---

16 (1828) 2 Hagg. 209.
17 Ibid 217–218.
18 Rose FD (n 2) 14.
19 (1865) Br. Of Lush. 341, 347.
20 See below 37.

ultimately explains the award element of salvage awards. It also explains the contention of Rose that a 'potential detriment to commerce may similarly be a reason for discouraging salvage claims for a modest service [benefit]'.[21] This sentiment regarding public policy is also evident in United States' jurisprudence where, in *The Henry Ewbank*,[22] Story J noted that salvage was a question of combining 'private merit and individual sacrifices' with 'larger considerations of the public good of commercial liberality and of international justice'.[23] From an environment first perspective, of course, the current concern with environmental protection as an outcome of salvage operations was absent at this time.

Waddams has noted that maritime salvage 'has operated directly so as actually to impose ... obligations to pay rewards'.[24] However, this view might not be entirely accurate and even be somewhat misleading. He links the question of public policy with the right to claim salvage, which is questionable. As noted by Rose, public policy 'derives from the central purpose of encouraging salvage services by, ... inflating the salvors award'[25] rather than by imposing an obligation where none is otherwise assumed to exist. Essentially, the public policy of encouragement only comes into play once the right to claim an award has been established.

Therefore, while public policy is an important component in the determination of salvage awards, it cannot be said to provide the basis for the right to claim. This much is also borne out by the historical analysis of salvage, which illustrated, in the context of English law, that the right to claim salvage was primarily established by legislation. Looking at matters from a functional perspective, such legislation may be explained with reference to specific outcomes and policy considerations, but it is first and foremost the legislation that provided the basis for the right to claim salvage. In relation to environmental services within salvage operations, public policy also explains its inclusion in salvage law via the 1989 Salvage Convention. This introduction of an environmental outcome via the instrument confirms the idea of policy considerations not being a direct basis for the right to salvage or indeed the explanation for the right to an award in the first place. It is here where the second basis for salvage mentioned by Rose, namely benefits conferred, comes into play. This much is also clear from *The Henry Ewbank* and *The Fusilier,* both of which confirmed the public policy underpinnings

---

21 Rose FD (n 2) 15.
22 (1883) 11 Fed Cas. (Case No 6376) 116.
23 Ibid 1170.
24 Waddams S, *Dimensions of Private Law: Categories and Concepts in Anglo-American Legal Reasoning* (CUP, 2003) 215.
25 Rose FD, 9 *Oxford J. Legal Stud* (n 7) 176. Also see text to nn 19, 21, and 22 above.

of salvage, albeit in combination with direct benefits conferred.[26] Story J, in *The Henry Ewbank*, referred to this component as the 'private right' component of the mixed question that is salvage.

Benefits Conferred as the Basis for Salvage

The law of salvage reward salvors for the benefits they confer as an entitlement in equity.[27] For historical and jurisdictional reasons, these have been limited to benefits to property.[28] The conferred benefits, in turn, inform the liability of their recipient to pay or contribute to salvage awards. In this regard, 'each and every interest which has received a benefit from the salvage service provided must contribute'.[29]

Nevertheless, while case law[30] has alluded to this private right aspect of salvage, they have shed no further light on the exact nature or basis of it except for the reference to equity. Rose has suggested that the benefits received may be dealt with as a manifestation of the principle of unjust enrichment.[31] In this regard, he has noted the increasing extent to which salvage had come to be included within the modern law of restitution for unjust enrichment.[32] He noted further that, subject to particular rules applicable to the type of situation in hand, a defendant receiving a benefit at the

---

26 See text to nn 19 and 22 above.

27 See the Goring, above (n12) 252.

28 Ibid. The apparent piecemeal development of the body of law of salvage has been influenced by the parallel carving out of a distinct Admiralty jurisdiction in England. In this regard, Professor Rose has noted that 'the jurisdiction of the admiralty court originated as one over property which was within the geographical jurisdiction of the Lord High Admiral'. See also Rose FD, *Oxford J. Legal Stud.* (n 7) 167, 183. Chances would always be that a law of salvage developed within the context of Admiralty with its liberal adoption of civil law concepts would acquire a distinct identity. Also see Chapter 2 for the historical analysis of the law of salvage.

29 Rose FD, *Kennedy and Rose on Salvage* (n 2) 15.

30 See *The Fusilier* (1865) Br. Of Lush. 341 and *The Henry* Ewbank (1883) 11 Fed Cas. (Case No 6376).

31 Rose FD, *Kennedy and Rose on Salvage* (n 2).

32 Ibid 20. Professor Rose provides as an example of authors that include salvage within the modern law of restitution for unjust enrichment Goff R and Jones G, *The Law of Restitution* (London, 1966), Klippert G, *Unjust Enrichment* (Butterworth, Toronto, 1983), which is indeed correct. However, this categorisation of salvage within the law of unjustified enrichment has not been uniformly observed. Examples of authors that do not include salvage within the law of unjustified enrichment are Lord Wright, *Legal Essays and Addresses* (1939) Cambridge, Birks P, *Introduction to the Law of Restitution* (OUP, 1985), Virgo, *Principles of the Law of Restitution* (OUP, 1999), Burrows A, *The Law of Restitution* (3rd edn, OUP, 2011).

expense of the claimant, in circumstances where he would be prima facie unjustly enriched, must make restitution to the claimant for it.[33]

An important aspect of Rose's suggestion is the fact that his enrichment analysis pertains specifically to the actual right to claim a salvage award. As such, it can be distinguished from the separate enquiry into the actual salvage award, which may be inflated for policy considerations.[34] It is also this latter aspect of salvage, the inflation of the award, which has given rise to the notion that salvage law is an exception to the general approach to restitutionary law, essentially an exclusively maritime permutation thereof.[35] Lord Bowen, in *Falcke,* albeit obiter, expressed the situation as follows:

> There is an exception to this proposition [that liabilities are not to be forced upon people behind their backs] in the maritime law. With regard to salvage ... the maritime law differs from the common law .... The maritime law, for the purposes of public policy and for the advantages of trade, imposes in these cases a liability upon the thing saved, a liability which is a special consequence arising out of the character of mercantile enterprises, the nature of sea perils, and the fact that the thing saved was saved under great stress and exceptional circumstances.[36]

Again, from the words of Lord Bowen, it is evident that the rules developed in salvage were likely consequential to the latter's placement in Admiralty with its property-based jurisdiction. As such, the availability of a remedy for one qualifying as a necessitous intervener seems to have depended on the forum within which a matter arose.[37] In this regard also, Aitken,[38] in commenting on the common law's aversion to providing a remedy to volunteers, has noted that it 'may be explained historically, and in particular, by examining the jurisdiction of those courts in which the volunteer ... [would be] accorded some courtesy'.[39] Of course, as noted in the preceding chapter, the Admiralty Court exercised an equitable jurisdiction with

---

33 Rose FD (n 2) 20.
34 Ibid.
35 Burrows A, *The Law of Restitution* (3rd edn OUP, Oxford, 2011) 469–476. Burrows provides instances of necessitous intervention and expressly includes salvage as an area where the English law provides the intervener a remedy. See also Virgo G, *The Principles of the Law of Restitution* (OUP, Oxford, 1999), Goff R and Jones G, *The Law of Restitution* (Sweet & Maxwell, London, 2007).
36 See above, n 13.
37 See Aitken, '*Negotiorum Gestio* and the Common Law: A Jurisdictional Approach' (1986–1988) *11 Sydney L. Rev* 566.
38 Ibid.
39 Ibid 566.

flexibility in its administration.[40] This explains the adoption of a body of salvage rules in line with the civil law *negotiorum gestio*,[41] which translates into English as the management of another's affairs or 'management of business'.[42] In this regard also, Rose has suggested that 'the law of salvage is the leading paradigm of English law's admission of recovery for necessitous intervention and affords a developed scheme for implementing it'.[43]

Rose, noting the peculiarity of certain rules to the law of salvage, alludes to very practical reasons that make the identification of salvage with the general law of restitution a worthwhile exercise. In this regard, he refers to the availability of a greater body of authoritative guidance for the resolution of practical issues.[44] One such practical issue for the purpose of this study would be environmental services in the context of salvage operations. In this regard, an important question would be whether the necessitous intervention could possibly explain or provide a basis for the incorporation of environmental pursuits in the law of salvage or the remuneration of such pursuits? The answer to that would probably be no.

Such an extension would be difficult because property salvage, due to its peculiar context, is evidently regarded as an exception to the common law approach. Nevertheless, authors such as Goff and Jones have argued for the development of a general doctrine of necessitous intervention and endeavoured to provide a basic framework for such claims.[45] However, the English law, to date, contains no general doctrine of necessitous intervention.[46] Therefore, the common law relating to necessitous intervention cannot be

40 Rose FD, *9 Oxford J. Legal Stud* (n 7) 167, 171.
41 Ibid. Prof Rose notes that '[t]he civil law, together with other sources, has also provided the foundation of the maritime law of salvage administered on similar principles, albeit as part of different national jurisdictions, by the admiralty courts of England and Scotland'. At 170. In *The Goring* [1987] 2 ALL ER 246 at 249, Sir Donaldson MR, noted that 'the Lord High Admiral ... administered a law of his own derived in part from such outlandish sources ... as the Roman law, the Rolls of Oléron ... and what seemed appropriate to Mediterranean trading nations'. At 249. See also Aitken (n 37). Aitken in providing a jurisdictional explanation for remedies in cases such as bills of exchange, burial, and salvage, regards the forum in which they were heard as paramount. Thus he states that these 'courts were under the control of judges whose training and outlook was pre-eminently civilian [and that] [i]t is no surprise if examples of *negotiorum gestio* should survive in such an environment, away from the encroachment of the common law'. At 568.
42 See *Committeri v Club Méditerranée SA (t/a Club Med Business)* [2018] EWCA Civ 1889 [2018] EWCA Civ 1889 para 22.
43 Rose FD, *9 Oxford J. Legal Stud* (n 7), 171.
44 Rose FD, *Kennedy and Rose on Salvage* above (n 2) 21.
45 Ibid.
46 *The Goring*, above (n 12) at 254-255. See also Goff and Jones (n 32), where the authors express regret that the English law contains no general doctrine of necessitous intervention. Para 17-026, 467. The authors also doubt whether, aside from the recognised exceptions such as salvage, 'English law will recognise other claims'. Para 17-008, 453.

used as the theoretical foundation for environmental services within salvage operations.

Of course, from an environmentalist perspective, one must acknowledge that environmental protection in the context of salvage operations confers a benefit on all, being for the common good and in furtherance of a broader social interest. Nevertheless, while coastal States may intervene in salvage operations,[47] to ensure the furthering of environmental outcomes, the key legal relationship in the law of salvage is between the salvor and owners of salved property.[48] As such, from the perspective of necessitous intervention, given the private legal relationships in salvage operations, there would be no management of the relevant parties' affairs. In this regard, one may again also refer to the words of Lord Mustill in *The Nagasaki Spirit*,[49] who noted that 'the owners of those [property] interests, who had to bear any salvage award that was made, had no financial stake in the protection of anything else'.[50] The conferred benefit, and the relevant management of affairs, would fall outside of the traditional salvage matrix.

Salvage, as an exception to the common law approach to necessitous intervention, represents a broader iteration of restitution for necessitous intervention, given that salvage awards are inflated for policy reasons. This is also why Rose has described salvage as the 'leading paradigm of English law's admission of recovery for necessitous intervention'[51] that 'affords a developed scheme for implementing it'.[52] Given this status of salvage as an exception and more developed instance of necessitous intervention, it must be pointed out that any development of necessitous intervention to account for environmental services would likely fall short of what is already available within the system of property salvage law.

This much is also borne out by the manner in which the 1989 Salvage Convention introduced remuneration for environmental services into the fabric of salvage law, only allowing salvors to claim their expenses.[53] This falls significantly short of property awards that may be inflated for policy reasons.[54] While one could explain the extent to which the law of salvage came to reflect environmental values in salvage operations with reference to public policy, one cannot comfortably explain these services with

---

47 See discussion below, 70 ff.
48 See discussion of the Salvage Convention in Chapter 4.
49 See above (n 9).
50 Ibid 327.
51 Rose FD, 9 Oxford J. Legal Stud (n 7) 171. See also In *ENE Kos 1 Ltd v Petroleo Brasiliero SA (No 2), The Kos* [2012] UKSC 17, [2012] 4 All ER 1 paras 19-20.
52 Rose FD, 9 *Oxford J. Legal Stud* (n 7), 171.
53 See discussion of Article 14 of the Salvage Convention below.
54 See discussion of Article 14 of the Salvage Convention and *The Nagasaki Spirit* below.

reference to necessitous intervention. Moreover, given the extent to which salvage law is viewed as a question involving both public policy and private rights,[55] environmental services do not fully align with the underpinning bases of salvage law.

Concluding Remarks

Given that the theoretical underpinnings of salvage law were developed within the limiting confines of property, legislation or a Convention would have been required to incorporate environmental values and outcomes into the law of salvage. Without the necessary legislative mandate, it is inconceivable that any judge would be able or willing to extend salvage and its elements to include the environment without encroaching on legislative prerogative in relation to the making of law. The extent to which salvage law represents the outer limits of necessitous intervention also renders this basis inappropriate for expanding the constituent elements of salvage law to include the environment.[56] Such an expansion could only ever be achieved by using legislation. The next chapter will examine the 1989 Salvage Convention, which represents a supra-national attempt to address environmental outcomes in salvage operations.

Bibliography

Aitken, '*Negotiorum Gestio* and the Common Law: A Jurisdictional Approach' (1986–1988) 11 Sydney L. Rev 566

Birks P, *Introduction to the Law of Restitution* (OUP 1985)

Burrows A, *The Law of Restitution* (3rd edn, OUP 2011)

Goff R and Jones G, *The Law of Restitution* (Sweet & Maxwell 1966)

Klippert G, *Unjust Enrichment* (Butterworth 1983)

Lord Wright of Durley, *Legal Essays and Addresses* (CUP 2014)

Reeder J, *Brice on Maritime Salvage* (4th edn, Sweet & Maxwell 2003)

Rose, *Kennedy and Rose on Salvage* (7th edn, Thomson Reuters (Legal) Limited 2010)

Rose FD, 'Restitution for the Rescuer' (1989) 9 Oxford J. Legal Stud. 167

Shaw R, 'The 1989 Salvage Convention and English Law' (1996) 2 L.M.C.L.Q 202

Virgo, *Principles of the Law of Restitution* (OUP 1999)

Waddams S, *Dimensions of Private Law: Categories and Concepts in Anglo-American Legal Reasoning* (CUP 2003)

---

55 See discussion of *The Fusilier* (n 19) and *The Henry Ewbank* (n 22) above.

56 In the South African case, *Transnet Limited t/a National Ports Authority v The MV Cleopatra Dream and The Cargo Laden on Board* (163/10) [2011] ZASCA 12 (11 March 2011), the court made short shrift of an attempt by counsel to introduce *negotiorum gestio* as a potential basis for a salvage claim in which the voluntariness of the operation was in issue. The court also noted doubts expressed in English law about the derivation of salvage from *negotiorum gestio*.

4 The International Convention on Salvage 1989 and the Environment

From the preceding chapter, it is evident that a change to the common law to better encompass environmental outcomes would always represent a real challenge. However, as shown by the historical analysis of salvage, legislation would be the simplest if not only way to expand upon the reach of salvage law to facilitate environmental protection as a fundamental concern. The 1989 International Convention on Salvage was the international community's attempt to align the law of salvage with environmental outcomes.

In a clear endorsement of the functional use of law, the Convention's preamble highlights 'increased concern for the protection of the environment' and the 'major contribution which efficient and timely salvage operations can make to the safety of vessels and other property in danger and to the protection of the environment'.[1] Thus, the Convention added protection of the environment as an outcome of salvage operations by ensuring 'that adequate incentives are available to persons who undertake salvage operations in respect of vessels and other property in danger'.[2] These incentives entail potentially larger salvage awards or, at least, the recovery of salvage expenses.[3] The Convention also imposes environmentally relevant duties and superimposes public law provisions on the essentially private law relationship between salvors and property owners, such as Article 9, which enshrines the rights of coastal States to protect their coastlines from pollution following maritime casualties.[4]

This chapter commences with an overview of some of the Convention's key definitions that are relevant to its environmental protection aims. This serves to demonstrate how the drafters of the instrument steered clear of

---

1 Preamble to the 1989 Salvage Convention.
2 Ibid.
3 See below for a discussion of Articles 13 and 14 of the London Convention, p 45 ff.
4 See discussion below, p 72 ff.

DOI: 10.4324/9781003315506-5

encroaching upon the traditional understanding of salvage operations. This is followed by an overview of Articles 13 and 14, which provide the primary mechanisms for the encouragement of salvors in the form of financial incentives, and a discussion of the duties imposed on salvors in Article 8 and its environmental protection reach. Lastly, the chapter addresses the public provisions that were added to the Convention in furtherance of environmental protection outcomes to assess the extent to which the instrument has managed to integrate the broader social interest in environmental protection into the private law of salvage.

Ultimately, from an environmentalist perspective, this chapter will demonstrate that the drafters of the Convention were likely constrained by the property and commercial identity of salvage law. In this regard, they were either reluctant or simply unable to elevate environmental outcomes relative to the traditional commercial and property bias of salvage. For example, in relation to remuneration for environmental services, salvors are only allowed to claim their expenses, which fall short of property awards that may be inflated for policy reasons.[5] Moreover, in relation to the public law provisions, these appear to have been cosmetic rather than representing a serious attempt to elevate environmental protection outcomes relative to the property and commercial outcomes of salvage law.

Environmentally Relevant Definitions

The first definition that is of importance to the environmental protection designs of the Convention is the definition of 'salvage operations'. Article 1(a) of the Convention defines salvage as 'any act or activity undertaken to assist a vessel or any other property in danger in navigable waters or in any other waters whatsoever'. This definition makes no mention of the environment, which immediately positions any environmental protection designs as 'add-ons' to traditional property salvage. This aspect of the Convention, as will be shown in the next chapter, also explains the difficulties encountered by salvors seeking to claim under instruments outside of salvage law.[6]

The first substantive provision to directly address the environment after the preamble is Article 1(d). It defines the environment as 'substantial physical damage to human health or to marine life or resources in coastal or inland waters or areas adjacent thereto, caused by pollution, contamination,

---

5 See discussion of Article 14 of the Salvage Convention and *Semco Salvage & Marine Pte Ltd v Lancer Navigaton Co Ltd (The Nagasaki Spirit)* [1997] 1 Lloyd's Rep. 323 [HL] below.

6 See discussion below, p 81 ff.

fire, explosion, or similar major incidents'. This definition, read in isolation, amounts to an abrupt, almost loose standing, introduction of the environment. Nevertheless, it creates an expectation that the Convention will address issues concerning environmental damage, which is of course ultimately borne out by provisions that encourage salvors,[7] impose duties,[8] and seek to balance the private property and broader environmental outcomes of salvage.

However, unlike paragraphs (b) and (c) of Article 1, there is no obvious link, expressed or otherwise, between this paragraph (d) and the definition of salvage operations in paragraph (a) of this article. Therefore, there is no suggestion that the 'environment' as defined in paragraph (d), is a component of, or part of any possible definition of salvage. As such, 'salvage operations' are legally distinct from environmental services, the latter only becoming relevant in the performing of traditional 'salvage operations'. Lord Mustill, in *The Nagasaki Spirit*, noted as much:

> [T]he right to special compensation depends on the performance of 'salvage operations' which, as already seen, are defined by art 1(a) as operations to assist a vessel in distress. Thus, although art 14 is undoubtedly concerned to encourage professional salvors to keep vessels readily available, this is still for the purposes of a salvage, for which the primary incentive remains a traditional salvage award. The ... incentive is now made more attractive by the possibility of obtaining new financial recognition for conferring a new type of incidental benefit. Important as it is, the remedy under art 14 is subordinate to the reward under art 13, and its functions should not be confused by giving it a character too closely akin to salvage.[9]

This legal distinction between environmental services and property salvage operations also confirms the argument in the preceding chapter, that environmental services do not align with the theoretical underpinnings of salvage law. Therefore, while the drafters could literally have included environmental protection services in the very definition of salvage operations, they chose not to do so. This choice was likely due to the various interests that had to be satisfied in the negotiations leading up to the finalisation of

---

7 Articles 13 and 14.
8 Article 8.
9 *The Nagasaki Spirit* (n 5) 513.

the Convention,[10] potentially coupled with a reluctance to fundamentally change standard definitions traditionally employed in the law of salvage.

From a theoretical perspective, this separation and conservatism would undoubtedly satisfy any traditionalist partial to the historical property roots of salvage. From a traditional salvage perspective, the wholesale introduction of public environmental issues into the traditional fabric of salvage would arguably nullify the clear identity of salvage, established over its long history. At the same time, one may argue that this approach is contrary to a perspective in which the environment is regarded as of fundamental importance. Instead of amending core definitions of salvage law, the drafters elected to follow an approach in which the encouragement of salvors was premised upon the availability of added financial incentives.

Encouragement and Financial Incentives (Articles 13 and 14 of the Convention)

Articles 13 and 14 are the key provisions aimed at the encouragement of salvors to go to the assistance of vessels where there is a threat to the environment. Article 13(1), which expressly creates the link between the award and the encouragement of salvors, provides that

> [t]he reward shall be fixed with a view to encouraging salvage operations, taking into account the ... criteria without regard to the order in which they are presented.

Article 13 of the Convention then lists the criteria for the calculation of the traditional salvage award and adds the 'skill and efforts of salvors in preventing or minimizing damage to the environment'[11] as a criterion for the fixing of the award. Therefore, the 'skill and efforts of salvors in preventing or minimising damage to the environment' could see an increase in the potential salvage award. While the environment is added as an additional factor to those traditionally considered in the calculation of a property salvage award, the criterion is placed on an equal footing with the other in relation to the determination of the salvage award. Nevertheless, one might assume that the presence or degree of an environmental threat would presumably

---

10 See Gaskell, 'The 1989 Salvage Convention and the Lloyd's Open Form (LOF) Salvage Agreement 1990' (1991–1992) *16 Tul. Mar. L.J. 1, 63.*

11 Salvage Convention Article 13(1)(b).

inform the relevance of the criterion relative to the others. However, as noted by Rose, courts have typically 'eschewed the weighing of factors'.[12]

During the negotiation of the Convention, the question of the relationship between paragraph (b) and the other paragraphs of Article 13 was also considered and there appear to have been notable difficulties in quantifying the increase of salvage awards due to Article 13(b).[13] The Travaux Préparatoires of the Convention, commenting on the addition of paragraph (b) to the criteria in Article 13, mentions that the purpose was to

> allocate the compensation payable to the salvors in respect of services performed with a view to preventing or minimizing damages to the environment between the owners of the cargo and their insurers and the owners of the vessel and their liability insurers.[14]

This was supposed to represent a 'sound commercial compromise'.[15] Very importantly, however, and indicative of the importance of environmental protection as an outcome, the Comité Maritime International (CMI) expressed the idea that the purpose behind Articles 13 and 14 was less to ensure a viable salvage industry than 'to cope with environmental problems alone'.[16] However, this being said, it is apparent that practical commercial considerations played a significant role in the deliberations. This is clear from the involvement of insurers in negotiations leading up to the Convention and the fact that express mention was made of the fact that 'in a salvage situation ... it is not the owners of such interests, but the insurers who bear the risk of economic loss and who derive the economic benefits from successful salvage operations'.[17]

---

12 Rose FD, *Kennedy and Rose on Salvage* (7th edn Thomson Reuters (Legal) Ltd, London (2010) 698.

13 The Travaux Préparatoires of the Convention on Salvage 1989, *Comité Maritime International, 295 at 353* www.comitemaritime.org/Travaux-Pr%C3%A9paratoires/0 ,27126,112632,00.html accessed 12 February 2022.

14 The Travaux Préparatoires of the Convention on Salvage 1989, *Comité Maritime International, 295.* www.comitemaritime.org/Travaux-Pr%C3%A9paratoires/0,27126 ,112632,00.html accessed 12 February 2022.

15 Ibid Document LEG 54/7 in The Travaux Préparatoires, 329.

16 The Travaux Préparatoires (n 13) 353. The CMI is a non-governmental not-for-profit international organisation tasked with the international unification of maritime law (see the CMI website http://comitemaritime.org) that undertook a review of the private law of salvage at the request of the International Maritime Organisation (IMO). It submitted a draft text that after consideration at the diplomatic conference in London became the 1989 Salvage Convention (See the Foreword to the Travaux Préparatoires).

17 Ibid 16.

While these practical considerations are understandable, the sentiments, from a legal perspective, might be misplaced. From a legal perspective, insurers' duty to pay is the result of a contractual undertaking. What the considerations, however, appear to do is to conflate two entirely different subjective rights, namely, the extent of the contractual undertaking of the insurer to its client and rights emanating from salvage operations. Essentially, what has happened was to include a practically related but legally irrelevant duty into the legal relationship between a salvor and the recipient of salvage services.

It is entirely logical to think that insurers pay only to the extent that they are legally bound by the contractual relationship between themselves and their clients. Moreover, this inclusion may be said to be removed from the third-party (public) interests in environmental protection in that the idea of remuneration is linked to the interests of the insurers involved, notably P&I and Hull and Machinery and apportionment as between them. In this way, any potential award is automatically linked only to the interests of the owners of salved property.

While related to the payment of special compensation under Article 14, the argument that 'insurers of ship and cargo cannot reasonably be required to cover fully the expenses for salvage operations from which another group of insurers – the liability insurers – regularly benefits', is a curious imposition that is based entirely on commercial sentiment and not law.[18] While one may accept that the appropriate division of payment as between different insurers will provide a more equitable distribution of the overall cost of salvage, this is an issue that should be addressed within the law of insurance. In the insurance context, the issue can conceivably be regulated with the appropriate contractual clauses.

Returning to Article 13(1)(b), it can be argued that Article 13(1)(b), being one of the factors to be taken into account in the determination of the appropriate salvage award, does not elevate environmental protection relative to the traditional concerns of salvage.[19] Nevertheless, the practical consequence of salvage operations mindful of this factor will be increased salvage awards and indirectly the protection of the environment.[20] In this manner environmental protection is positioned, indirectly, via financial incentives, as an outcome of salvage operations. This is in line with the

---

18 Travaux Préparatoires, above n 13.

19 In *Semco Salvage and Marine Pte Ltd v Lancer Navigation Co Ltd (The Nagasaki Spirit)* [1997] 1 ALL ER 502, at 505, Lord Mustill held that 'the services performed remain, as they have always been, services to ship and cargo, and the award is borne by those standing behind ship and cargo'.

20 Ibid.

observations in the preceding chapter of encouragement as a matter of public policy, which is regarded as being at the root of, or as the basis of salvage law.[21]

While environmental outcomes are likely promoted, even if only indirectly so, by the addition of Article 13(b), it is one of several criteria, with no real clarity about its ranking relative to the other criteria. As such, one can only speculate regarding its relative weight. From an environmentalist perspective, although there is a possibility of increased awards and the protection of the environment is positioned as an outcome of the law of salvage, even if only indirectly so, Article 13(1)(b) does not position the environment as a primary concern.[22] Perhaps, given its history and the development of principles and definitions along the lines of property and commercial interests, it is too much to ask of the law of salvage to accommodate the more recent concern with the environment in a manner that would satisfy the environmentalist.

These very difficulties probably explain the drafting of Article 14 of the Convention, which embodies the move away from the traditional no-cure-no-pay principle of salvage law, to facilitate an interest, the environment and its protection, that was never within the matrix of interests of property salvage. Article 14 allows a salvor carrying out salvage operations in respect of a vessel, which by itself or its cargo threaten damage to the environment, to recover at least its expenses in the form of special compensation.[23] However, special compensation is triggered only when a salvor undertakes property salvage operations that pose a threat to the environment.

Therefore, special compensation only arises in respect of salvors carrying out traditional salvage operations, where the same property threatens the environment. Constructed in this way, environmental protection services and their compensation are evidently secondary to property salvage operations. While this makes sense in view of the historical property bias of salvage operations and the law of salvage, it does not align with growing environmental protection preferences. At the same time, it is difficult to imagine how matters could be ordered differently, given that maritime incidents triggering property salvage operations are as a matter of cause antecedent to environmental protection concerns.

---

21 See Chapter 2. Also, see Rose FD (n 12) 14.

22 In *The Nagasaki Spirit* (n 5) at 505, Lord Mustill held that 'the services performed remain, as they have always been, services to ship and cargo, and the award is borne by those standing behind ship and cargo'.

23 Article 14(1).

Despite the obvious broader social benefits consequential upon the addition of special compensation to the law of salvage, Article 14(1) provides that the salvor is 'entitled to special compensation from the owner of [the] vessel'. Therefore, to be consistent with the salvage notion that 'each and every interest which has received a benefit ... must contribute',[24] a benefit must have been conferred on such an owner. Here, the obvious benefit would be a shipowner's potential liability for environmental damage caused, with broader social implications purely incidental thereto.

Therefore, Article 14, by virtue of its wording, is primarily directed at the individual interests of shipowners and principally geared towards prioritising the broader interest in the development of trade. This, despite the environmental aims of the Convention, appears to be restrictive, albeit consistent with a traditional understanding of salvage. Special compensation, although not expressed as such, appears to be premised on the limited notion of averting potential shipowner liability, suggesting unwillingness on the part of the drafters of the Convention to fully integrate environmental services incidental to property salvage operations into the law of salvage. Of course, even if there is the willingness to do this, one must be mindful of the fact that this might impact the traditionally established reach and purpose of salvage law.

Despite the obvious public benefit conferred by salvors, Article 14(1) makes it clear that the salvor is 'entitled to special compensation from the owner of [the] vessel'. Why would it be the case that special compensation is only payable by the owner of the vessel and not cargo interests or perhaps other interests? This is the case despite benefits conferred outside of the traditional salvage matrix. If one accepts as a central tenet of the law of salvage that 'each and every interest which has received a benefit from the salvage service provided must contribute',[25] why should Article 14 single out the vessel owner to pay special compensation?

First, the liability of the vessel owner to pay this award must be predicated upon the fact that a benefit of some kind had been bestowed. In this regard, it is difficult to imagine any benefit to the vessel owner other than its potential liability for environmental damage caused. Nevertheless, benefits conferred may exceed such liability. Second, and implicit to the acknowledgement of conferred benefits resulting in an award, is that cargo owners or other third parties must have received no benefit or a benefit not worthy of recognition under the Convention. Here again, in relation to cargo owners, any potential benefit could only be in relation to their potential

---

24   See Chapter 3, n 142 and text thereto.
25   See Chapter 3, 75.

liability for damage caused, unless the containment of oil is simply regarded as an aspect of property rescue.

However, cargo interests typically do not incur liability for environmental damage as is the case with the shipowner. Therefore, there would be no benefit resulting in a duty to pay. This would certainly explain their exclusion from Article 14(1) special compensation. This results in an anomaly given that cargo owners are liable for an Article 13 award that includes consideration for 'the skill and efforts of the salvors in preventing or minimizing damage to the environment'.[26] What would be the benefit conferred upon cargo owners under Article 13(1)(b), over and above their property interest, given that there is no liability?

While, for the purpose of Article 14(1), one may accept that liability for environmental damage should attach to the shipowner only,[27] because of its operational role in the transportation of potentially polluting cargo,[28] it does not explain the liability of cargo owners pursuant to Article 13(1)(b). Moreover, arguments are consistent with the idea that no such distinction is to be entertained and that any enhancement of an award should be borne by all salved property rateably in accordance with salved values.[29] This is also expressly confirmed by Article 13(2). The result here is that special compensation, by excluding cargo owners due to their not having received a benefit, is more in line with a central tenet of salvage than the Article 13(1)(b) situation.

Another issue raised by Article 14(1) singling out the shipowner, is that benefits bestowed on interests outside of the traditional salvage matrix such as coastal States are not considered for the purpose of special compensation. While it appears to contradict the central tenet that involves payment for benefits conferred, it makes sense if one acknowledges and maintains the traditional notion of salvage as a service to maritime property only. In this regard, Brice has alluded to the fact that under existing salvage law it is only where the salvor has conferred a benefit that he is entitled to remuneration, but it is not everyone who benefits who is liable to reward him.[30] Essentially, while parties outside of private salvage relationship benefit, these are simply not relevant for the remuneration of salvors under Article 14(1) which imposes the duty to pay on the shipowner.

---

26 Article 13(1)(b).
27 See *The Velox* [1906] p 263.
28 Khee-Jin Tan A, *Vessel-Source Marine Pollution: The Law and Politics of International Regulation* (Cambridge OUP, 2006) 38.
29 See Reeder, *Brice on Maritime Salvage* (4th edn, Sweet & Maxwell, 2003) 411.
30 Ibid 418.

Some have raised questions regarding this apparent inequity with Witte suggesting that an appropriate remuneration system 'should be based on a more equitable sharing of responsibility for salvage costs'.[31] Gold, similarly, alludes to the fact that 'costs for this protection has to be spread equitably',[32] which the current scheme appears not to do. This might be because such remuneration is simply not regarded as salvage costs, which would also be consistent with the Convention's definition of salvage operations,[33] and a narrow conception of salvage.

Of course, while underpinned by public policy considerations, salvage is essentially a private law relationship between salvor and the owner of salved property. Any potential liability of a coastal State to pay for environmental services from which they benefit falls outside this private law relationship. The law of salvage, given its property bias, is simply not geared towards this public benefit. Brice has noted that 'the changes which have taken place in the nature of sea transport and the cargoes carried gave rise to problems which had ramifications both in public and in private law'.[34] Nevertheless, given the basic legal relationship between salvor and owner of salved property, it is difficult to see how any remuneration paid for environmental services by coastal States could be facilitated under the law of salvage, as well as the way this should be paid. Moreover, the liability of only the shipowner to pay for such remuneration appears at best to be a commercial compromise based on the ease with which such liability can be attached.[35]

Brice has also noted that beneficiaries, outside the traditional salvage matrix, might not be easy to ascertain and that normal insurance would not cover such a payment in so far as it exceeded that which was payable under a customary form of marine insurance upon ship, cargo, and freight.[36] As such, the idea of benefits conferred resulting in remuneration appears to be partially absent in relation to both Articles 13 and 14. Brice also notes that 'neither the owners nor the underwriters of ship, cargo and freight would wish to pay for benefits, perhaps of a very substantial nature, conferred upon third parties, certainly not more than the normal enhancement envisaged

31 Witte A, 'LOF and Defence of the Marine Environment' www.marine-salvage.com/media-information/conference-papers/isus-associate-members-day-april-2008 accessed 2 September 2021.

32 Gold E 'Marine Salvage: Towards a New Regime' (1989) 20 *J. Mar. L. & Com* 487, 503.

33 Salvage Convention Article 1(a).

34 (n 29).

35 Kee-Jin Tan A (n 28).

36 Brice on Salvage (n 29) 419.

in making awards of salvage remuneration in the customary manner.'[37] Therefore, it appears as if the very legal theoretical structure of salvage precludes any real possibility of an award within salvage that would represent a fair spreading of the costs for such remuneration among all that benefit.

Should one wish to explain the shipowner's liability to pay under Article 14(1) in a manner consistent with the twin bases of salvage, then it must be that this liability arises because a benefit has been conferred. The extent to which other beneficiaries are excluded will, nevertheless, be consistent with the idea expressed by Brice that 'it is not everyone who benefits who is liable to reward'[38] the salvor. This, despite the clear environmental aims of the Convention, appears to be quite restrictive, albeit consistent with a traditional understanding of salvage. This also appears to conflict with the pursuit of environmental protection outcomes and the equitable remuneration of salvors. Special compensation, while not expressed as such, is clearly structured on the unduly limited notion of averting potential shipowner liability, suggesting an unwillingness on the part of the drafters of the Convention to fully integrate environmental services incidental to property salvage operations into the law of salvage.

Penalties and Environmental Protection

In addition to the incentives contained in Articles 13 and 14, the Convention contains further provisions that indicate an increased concern with environmental protection. The Convention uses both the positive encouragement provided by Articles 13 and 14 and the imposition of duties and penalties to reflect and bolster the underlying 'environmental protection concerns' alluded to in the preamble.

Article 14, besides its encouragement of environmental services, sees an imposition of what appears to be a penalty on the salvor whose actions impede the minimising or averting of environmental damage. In this regard Article 14(5) of the Convention provides:

> If the salvor has been negligent and has thereby failed to prevent or minimize damage to the environment, he may be deprived of the whole or part of any special compensation due under this Article.

The addition of this penalty appears to detract from the encouragement value of Article 14 and the Convention generally. However, one could argue that

37 Ibid 418.
38 Ibid.

the addition of Article 14(5) serves to maximise the potential environmental benefits of salvage services. The possibility of special compensation encourages salvors to render salvage services in circumstances where environmental protection is a priority. However, Article 14(5) ensures that they act in a manner that promotes the attaining of this outcome. The environmental protection aims of the Convention are thus bolstered through the employment of positive encouragement while conduct that may impact negatively upon environmental protection is discouraged.

In the absence of the provision contained in Article 14(5), it would theoretically be possible for a salvor to claim expenses despite conduct that may actively prevent the averting or minimising of environmental damage. Article 14(1) only requires salvage services in relation to a vessel 'which by itself or its cargo threatened damage to the environment' and the failure of the salvor to 'earn a reward under Article 13 at least equivalent to the special compensation' of Article 14.[39] Therefore, one could have a salvor recover expenses despite behaviour that would be considered contrary to the environmental protection aims of the Convention. One could possibly argue that such environmentally negative conduct by a salvor would fall foul of Article 18 of the Convention.[40] However, as will be shown, this article by itself is not the ideal way to deal with conduct that may prevent the minimising or prevention of environmental damage.

In terms of Article 14(5), conduct of the salvor that may defeat the object of environmental protection only impacts upon special compensation or a part of such special compensation. This may appear excessively lenient for the punishing of conduct contrary to the environmental aims of the Convention. However, it might bolster the centrality and the ultimate attainment of environmental protection. Any attempt to link 'environmentally negligent conduct' to an Article 13 salvage award could arguably defeat the public policy pertaining to the encouragement of salvors.

Salvors are, therefore, encouraged to go to the assistance of the environment without fear of legal technicalities that could render their salvage efforts a financial disaster. While the possibility of the enhancement of special compensation would encourage conduct conducive to environmental protection, Article 14(5) would discourage conduct that may prevent it. This reading of Article 14(5) informs the earlier assertion that Article 18, by itself, is not ideal for the furthering of the environmental protection credentials of the Convention. In order to effectively further the environmental aims of the Convention, Articles 14(5) and 18 are both necessary.

39 See above 48–50.
40 See below, p 54.

Despite the argument offered about Article 14(5) encouraging appropriate conduct on the part of salvors, questions regarding its necessity have been raised. Professor Rose has suggested that the article might be superfluous in view of the provisions contained in Article 18 of the Convention.[41]

> A salvor may be deprived of the whole or part of the payment due under this Convention to the extent that the salvage operations have become necessary or more difficult because of fault or neglect on his part or if the salvor has been guilty of fraud or other dishonest conduct.

Professor Rose argues that Article 14(5) is superfluous because the special compensation provided under Article 14 is included in the word 'payment' used in Article 18.[42] He argues that the only practical function of Article 14(5), 'if any, is to emphasise that one of the types of misconduct mentioned in the more widely drafted article may have the effect of reducing or eliminating a potential award of special compensation'.[43] Professor Gaskell similarly alludes to the possibility of Article 14(5) being superfluous because of Article 18, without a firm statement to that effect.[44] However, the aforementioned views, especially that of Professor Rose, are too reliant on the single word 'payment'.

Why would the drafters of the Convention insist on an additional Article 14(5), or indeed an Article 18, if the two are essentially addressing the same issue? The need for both articles becomes apparent if one interprets them with reference to their respective underlying purposes and against the overall purpose of the Convention (as a whole). This would be consistent with the approach of Lord Mustill in *The Nagasaki Spirit*. The Judge, in interpreting the relevant provisions of the Convention, read the words 'in the general context of the new regime'.[45] In this regard, Lord Mustill also alluded to the correctness of an approach that pays heed to the history of the Convention.[46] Lord Mustill, therefore, commenced his interpretation with the wording of the Convention 'in the general context of the ... regime'.[47]

If one follows the approach endorsed by the House of Lords in *The Nagasaki Spirit*, one has to interpret Article 14(5) in context. In this regard, the immediate context of the article would be that of the entire article.

---

41 See Rose FD (n 12) 226. Also see Gaskell, 16 *Tul. Mar. L.J. 1, 63* (n 10).

42 Ibid.

43 Ibid.

44 Gaskell 16 *Tul. Mar. L.J.* (n 10).

45 *The Nagasaki Spirit* (n 5) 512.

46 Ibid.

47 Ibid.

Thus, the idea of special compensation and the policy underpinnings of the scheme ought to be instructive in any interpretation of Article 14(5). In this regard, Brice notes that 'what Article 14 was seeking to do was to give salvors extra encouragement'.[48] The aforesaid extra encouragement, as mentioned before, is in the form of the 'special compensation' where salvors render services in a situation that may otherwise have been economically unattractive.

While Article 14 encourages salvors to direct their attention at the averting or minimising of environmental harm, it also underpins the general concern with environmental protection as established in the preamble of the Convention. In this regard, scholarly opinion has suggested that environmental protection was the *raison d'être* for the Convention. In the words of Brice, the 'underlying purpose of the London Convention was to encourage and to some extent compel salvors to take action during the course of salvage operations to protect the environment'.[49] Therefore, any contextual reading of Articles 14, 14(5), and 18 of the Convention demands that one pays attention to the environmental concerns embodied by the Convention as a whole.

Of course, at first blush, a literal reading of Articles 14(5) and 18 does appear to support the view that the former is superfluous because of the latter's provisions. For example, the term 'payment' as used in Article 18 would be wide enough to cover the special compensation awarded under Article 14. However, in terms of Article 18, a salvor 'may be deprived of the whole or part of the payment due under this Convention'. Thus, a salvor could potentially lose the whole, or a part of, the traditional salvage where his actions necessitate salvage operations or make commenced operations more difficult. Therefore, the sanction contained in Article 18 goes further than that of Article 14(5). In contrast, negligent conduct by a salvor in terms of Article 14(5) only impacts upon the special compensation component of payment under the Convention. This formulation, arguably, serves to promote the encouragement of salvors while keeping their conduct honest in relation to environmental protection.

---

48 Brice on Maritime Salvage (n 29) 444. This line of argument was also followed by Mr Brice QC, as he then was, pointing out to the court in *The Nagasaki Spirit* that 'the explicit purpose of the new salvage regime ... in the words of the preamble [is] to provide "adequate incentives" to keep themselves in readiness to protect the environment'. Lord Mustill regarded this the teleological method proposed by Mr Brice as correct.

49 Ibid. While the use of the word 'compel' might prove to be somewhat strong, the idea of environmental protection nevertheless finds expression through its addition to the duties imposed on salvors and owners by the Convention. See discussion of Article 8 below, 59.

The contention that Article 14(5) is superfluous or subsumed under Article 18 fails to explain the problem of the latter taking away that (the penalty being limited to the special compensation part of payment) which is given under the former. Moreover, the notion that Article 14(5) is subsumed under Article 18 is not consistent with the overall environmental aims of the Convention. So, how is one to explain the inclusion of both these articles? One could, both on a literal and teleological reading, explain the need for both these articles, thereby furthering the overall environmental protection aims of the Convention.

While the term 'payment' serves as the basis for the argument that Article 14(5) is superfluous, other terms, together with a teleological reading of the provisions, appear to point in a different direction. Firstly, the use of the term 'salvage operation' in Article 18 distinguishes it from Article 14(5). 'Salvage operation' is defined in Article 1(a) of the Convention as 'any act or activity undertaken to assist a vessel or any other property in danger in navigable waters or in any other waters whatsoever'.

Thus, it would appear as if the mischief address by Article 18 is different from that of Article 14(5). The latter makes no mention of 'salvage operations' but, instead, regulates negligent conduct in relation to the prevention and minimising of environmental damage. A 'salvage operation' is distinct from environmental services with the latter only becoming an issue in the performing of the traditional 'operation'. In this regard, the words of Lord Mustill in *The Nagasaki Spirit* may once more prove to be instructive.

> [T]he right to special compensation depends on the performance of 'salvage operations' which, as already seen, are defined by art 1(a) as operations to assist a vessel in distress. Thus, although art 14 is undoubtedly concerned to encourage professional salvors to keep vessels readily available, this is still for the purposes of a salvage, for which the primary incentive remains a traditional salvage award. The only structural change in the scheme is that the incentive is now made more attractive by the possibility of obtaining new financial recognition for conferring a new type of incidental benefit. Important as it is, the remedy under art 14 is subordinate to the reward under art 13, and its functions should not be confused by giving it a character too closely akin to salvage.[50]

The words of Lord Mustill, when applied to Articles 14(5) and 18, suggest a definite difference in focus. The former introduces new 'financial

---

50 *The Nagasaki Spirit* (n 126) 513.

recognition' for conferring a 'new type of incidental benefit', which can be described as the 'environmental services' that are rendered where a marine disaster poses an environmental risk. While environmental services and the award of special compensation in terms of Article 14 are linked to the performance of salvage operations, the former is not synonymous with the latter in a legal technical sense. Thus, fault or neglect, fraud, and other dishonest conduct in relation to salvage operations, as provided for in Article 18, are distinguishable from negligence in relation to the minimising or averting of damage to the environment. This reading allows an effective explanation for the two articles, which also better serves the underlying purpose of the Convention.

On Professor Rose's argument, one might assume that Article 14(5) could be removed without significantly impacting upon the reading of Article 18. However, the extent to which one could distinguish between 'salvage operations' as defined in Article 1 and the 'environmental services' contemplated by Article 14 would still leave the problem of explaining how the former could include the latter. Notwithstanding the wide definition of 'payment' in Article 18, it is difficult to see how one could get around the limited confines of 'salvage operations' as defined in Article 1(a) of the Convention.

On a teleological reading of the provisions, the argument for a distinction between Articles 14(5) and 18 gains further ground. As mentioned, Article 14 generally serves to encourage salvors to apply their minds to the minimising or averting of environmental damage. However, the absence of Article 14(5) might potentially have the exact opposite effect. It is difficult to imagine how a salvor could be encouraged to engage in environmental services when fault could potentially result in the loss of the complete salvage award. Therefore, the view of Professor Rose that the article is superfluous might not be mindful of the aims of the Convention while also not being sensitive to the difference in the aims of the provisions. Article 14(5) deals with conduct in relation to environmental services while Article 18 deals with 'salvage operations' as defined by Article 1 of the Convention. While intimately linked, these concepts are not synonymous. Given the general policy underpinnings of the Convention and especially insofar as it relates to the encouragement of salvors to minimise or prevent damage to the environment, Articles 14(5) and 18 are best kept as distinct and separate provisions.

One appropriately drafted provision could possibly take care of the concerns raised. However, such a provision would have to be drafted with the legal technical limitations of the Convention in mind. Moreover, it must be appreciated that the attachment of Article 18 consequences to environmental services might have a negative impact on the encouragement of salvors. Such a provision, therefore, must similarly distinguish between the penalties as provided for in Articles 14(5) and 18. As such, the regulation of the salvor's conduct in relation to environmental services, to the extent that it is incorporated into the Convention, is better dealt with in a paragraph of the provision specifically dealing with the issue of special compensation and the averting or minimising of damage to the environment.

Duties and Environmental Protection

According to some academic authors,[51] Article 8 of the Convention imposes an environmental protection duty on salvors. Gaskell, in an analysis of the article, expressly mentions the 'four duties of the salvor'[52] that are listed in Article 8(1)(a)–(d). However, while Gaskell's reading of a distinct environmental protection duty on salvors might be consistent with a teleological understanding of the Convention, it is not supported by a literal reading of the article itself. In order to fully explain this latter aspect, it is necessary to set out the full text of Article 8(1)(a)–(d):

1 The salvor shall owe a duty to the owner of the vessel or other property in danger:

   (a) to carry out the salvage operations with due care;

   (b) in performing the duty specified in subparagraph (a), to exercise due care to prevent or minimise damage to the environment;

   (c) whenever circumstances reasonably require, to seek assistance from other salvors; and

   (d) to accept the intervention of other salvors when reasonably requested to do so by the owner or master of the vessel or other property in danger; provided however that the amount of his reward shall not be prejudiced should it be found that such a request was unreasonable.

Clear from a reading of Article 8(1), the exercise of due care to prevent or minimise damage to the environment in paragraph (b) is formulated with reference to the duty 'to carry out the salvage operations with due care' in (a).[53] In this manner, Article 8(1)(b) is a qualifier to the duty contained in Article 8(1)(a) rather than a separate duty. The phrasing of paragraph (b)

---

51 See Gaskell N (n 10) and Allen M, 'The International Convention on Salvage and LOF 1990' (1991) 22 *J. Mar. L. & Com.* 119.

52 Gaskell N (n 10), 42.

53 Article 8(1)(a).

and its express reference to Article 8(1)(a) precludes the possibility of it being separate and distinct from the latter. Thus, one might also read paragraph (b) as an informative component to the duty contained in Article 8(1)(a). On this understanding, a failure to exercise due care in relation to the protection of the environment would almost amount to an improperly discharged Article 8(1)(a) duty. Of course, this reading would not necessarily contradict the assumption of a fundamental environmental protection norm in that one might explain paragraph (b) 'duty' as a necessary component to the exercise of the actual duty contained in paragraph (a). However, there are no cases of the article being interpreted in this manner.

De la Rue has suggested that it is only in performing the salvage operations that the salvor is under any duty of care to prevent or minimise pollution.[54] The author also noted that

> [w]hilst this duty may … affect the manner in which he carries out any act or activity undertaken to assist a vessel or any other property in danger, it does not impose on him any obligation to engage in preventative or clean-up measures unconnected with such assistance.[55]

De la Rue's view on the relationship between paragraphs (b) and (a) is, on a literal reading of Article 8, consistent with the actual wording of the section. It is also consistent with the earlier noted legal distinction between environmental services and salvage operations and the earlier noted idea of environmental protection as subsidiary and secondary to property salvage operations. On a balance of importance, as it stands, Article 8 prevents any possibility of free-standing environmental protection efforts not connected with property salvage, which suggests a clear priority in salvage for traditional property and commercial outcomes.

The Article 8 duty is also owed to the 'owner of the vessel or other property in danger', which casts the environmental protection aspect thereof as being in furtherance of private interests. Even if not read in this way, one would have to ask why the broader social interest in environmental

---

54 De La Rue, *Shipping and the Environment* (2nd edn, Informa, London, 2009).

55 Ibid. Also see, Liang Chen, 'Recent developments in the Law of Salvage of the Marine Environment' (2001) 16 *Int'l J. Marine & Coastal L.* 686. Dr Liang Chen, in commenting on environmental salvage and its subordinate nature to the traditional salvage of marine property notes that the 'subordinate nature … can also be seen clearly from the wording of Article 8(1)(b) which makes the duty of marine environmental salvage secondary to that of ordinary marine property salvage as provided in Article 8(1)(a)'. At 688. Of course, the reference to an environmental duty amounts to the creation of a separate duty which, as argued, does not follow from the wording of Article 8.

protection is provided for as purely incidental to private interests? Even if paragraph (b) is to be regarded as a separate duty owed to the owner of the vessel or other property, one must wonder about the extent of the benefit conferred. Surely, the recipients of property salvage services could not obtain a greater benefit from a free-standing environmental duty than the extent of their possible liability for environmental damage. Any suggestion that the benefit conferred could be more than this would take the duty beyond the wording of Article 8 as it would amount to more than 'a duty to the owner of the vessel or other property in danger'.

Essentially, environmental protection is added as a secondary concern to the traditional outcomes of salvage and directed at the prevention of liability on the part of the recipients of salvage services. As such, Article 8 is geared towards private commercial interests, which is accepted as having direct proportionality to the promotion of marine commerce. As such, from a social interest theory analysis and an environmentalist perspective, it is evident that the Salvage Convention has not elevated environmental outcomes *vis-à-vis* the traditional property and commercial outcomes of salvage law.

Public Provisions and Environmental Protection Outcomes

As mentioned, the preamble to the Convention acknowledges the role of salvors in a wider environmental protection matrix. Furthermore, the Convention was drafted mindful of legal factors outside its ambit that could impact efforts aimed at environmental protection. In this regard, specific mention must be made of Articles 5, 6, 9, and 11 of the Convention, which represent public law aspects of salvage law and environmental protection concerns. These articles, consistent with the aims of the Convention, express environmental protection ideals but, as will be demonstrated, do not interact seamlessly with the essentially private law nature and limitations of salvage law. However, they do stand as good indicators of the point Brice makes:

> Whereas until recent years a salvage service and the incident giving rise to it could only be expected to affect the salvor and the owner of ship, cargo and freight, the changes which have taken place in the nature of sea transport and the cargoes carried gave rise to problems which had ramifications both in public and in private law.[56]

---

56 Reeder J, *Brice on the Maritime Law of Salvage* (5th edn, Sweet & Maxwell, 2011).

Of course, Brice's view on the nature of the salvage service and the incident giving rise to it is correct when we consider the greening of salvage law and the extent to which coastal States may intervene in the interests of broader environmental interests. Nevertheless, the key issue of how this twin aspect of salvage operations ought to be regulated in law remains. An assessment of the public provisions of the Convention may shed further light on whether the Salvage Convention was a good choice for regulating environmental services in the context of salvage operation and their remuneration. Also, from a social theory and environmentalist perspective, this examination will assist in assessing the extent to which the Convention has managed to integrate and balance broader social concerns with the traditional law of salvage.

Article 5

Article 5 of the Convention, while not expressly concerned with the environment, nevertheless, impacts upon environmental protection issues as it pertains to 'salvage operations controlled by public authorities'.[57] In this regard, it is a given that coastal States would be concerned with the protection of their coastlines and that they would seek to involve themselves in or have some control over salvage operations where there is a threat of environmental damage. Such involvement will typically be through the agency of the appropriate public authorities.[58] For this reason, while the provision is not expressly linked to environmental services, it is clearly in furtherance, even if only indirectly so, of environmental protection by the acceptance of national legislation that may charge the appropriate public authority with environmental protection duties.

The Convention leaves the regulation of salvage operations performed by public authorities to the national legislation of coastal States.[59] However, insofar as the salvage operations are performed by private salvors under the control of such public authorities, their rights to a salvage award and any other rights of the salvor against the recipient of salvage services granted under the Convention are expressly retained.[60] Thus, while the coastal State may direct such private salvors, the salvors' rights against the owners of ship and cargo are not affected. Essentially, the services rendered by a private salvor will retain their nature as salvage services with the rights and

---

57 Article 5 of the Salvage Convention.
58 See Chapter 5.
59 Article 5(1) and (3).
60 Article 5(2).

duties flowing from salvage services. Prior to the Convention, such services, insofar as they are directed by public authorities, would not have amounted to salvage services as they would have lacked the required voluntariness.

Of course, this would not have precluded the coastal State from providing compensation to such a salvor in consideration for the environmental benefits received by the coastal State. The legal regulatory mechanism for such consideration in return for environmental services could conceivably be outside of the property confines of the law of salvage, such as a contract between the coastal State and salvors. In this regard, examples abound of contractual arrangements between coastal States and salvors, primarily aimed at environmental protection, that are not salvage contracts although they are not fully removed from the confines of salvage law.[61] However, despite this possible avenue of redress, environmental protection demands and assumptions regarding the ability of the traditional law of salvage to facilitate these demands has led to the variation of a standard requirement of the law of salvage through Article 5.[62]

The issue of potential conflict between the commercial aims of the salvor in discharging their Convention duties in relation to the owners of maritime property and the demands of coastal States in relation to environmental protection is not mentioned by Article 5. In this regard, it is obvious that the directions issued by coastal States may negatively impact upon the work of salvors and the absence of a mechanism to resolve this creates unnecessary uncertainty. In this regard, any further changes to the traditional law of salvage will only exacerbate the issue of uncertainty and we should explore options outside of the salvage law framework to address matters.

Article 9

Article 9 is another public law provision that provides for the rights of coastal States in the context of salvage operations in relation to environmental protection by subjecting the Convention and the rights it affords to

> the right of the coastal State concerned to take measures in accordance with generally recognized principles of international law to protect its coastline or related interests from pollution or the threat of pollution following upon a maritime casualty or acts relating to such a casualty

---

61 See discussion below, 70 ff of pre-arranged contracts involving the retention of salvage tugs on standby for the purpose of protecting the environment in marine casualties.

62 Where salvors are controlled by public authorities, they can avail themselves of the rights and remedies provided under the Convention.

which may reasonably be expected to result in major harmful consequences, including the right of a coastal State to give directions in relation to salvage operations.

This article essentially confirms the powers of intervention that coastal
States have in maritime casualties where there is a threat to the environment.
The United Kingdom's powers of intervention derive from certain public
international law instruments such as the Intervention Convention.[63] It
grants coastal States the right to take measures on the high seas as may
be necessary to prevent, mitigate, or eliminate grave and imminent danger
to their coastline or related interests from the pollution of the sea by oil
following upon a maritime casualty.[64] It also includes acts related to such
a casualty, which may reasonably be expected to result in major harmful
consequences.

However, Article V of the Intervention Convention provides some
restrictions on how the coastal State may exercise the powers conferred
under Article I. For e.g. measures must be 'proportionate to the damage
actual or threatened to it',[65] not exceed what is 'necessary to achieve the
ends' in Article I and not 'unnecessarily interfere with the rights and interests
of the flag State, third States and of any persons, physical or corporate,
concerned'.[66] While the Intervention Convention does not mention salvors,
they would on a literal reading be covered by the reference to 'persons,
physical or corporate'. How then, should this aspect of the Convention be
aligned with the idea that the rights provided in the Salvage Convention
are subject to the exercise of such powers of intervention? The only answer
here that will provide the proper recognition of environmental protection as
a fundamental concern would be that salvors should not be included under
Article V.

The Merchant Shipping Act 1995, in conferring powers on the Secretary
of State to give directions in salvage operations,[67] also expressly provides
for the instances in which such powers can be exercised. Referring as it

---

63 International Convention Relating to the Intervention on the High Seas in Cases of Oil
    Pollution Casualties, 1969. See also, Reeder J, *Brice on Maritime Law of Salvage* (n 56).
    The author notes that the Intervention Convention is 'in a sense enacted in ss. 137–140 of
    the Merchant Shipping Act 1995'. 449.
64 Article 1 of the International Convention Relating to the Intervention on the High Seas in
    Cases of Oil Pollution Casualties, 1969.
65 Article 5(1).
66 Article 5(2).
67 The Merchant Shipping Act 1995 ch II, s 137(2).

does to 'shipping casualties',[68] a salvage operation as the response to a casualty that involves a threat to the environment would be the type of situation where these powers will be exercised. Essentially, the opinion of the Secretary of State as to the urgency of the need to exercise the powers conferred is the way the right to intervene is triggered, which suggests a definite commitment to protecting and promoting the public interests in environmental protection relative to private salvage interests, albeit outside of the salvage law matrix.

However, one may ask how one should understand Article 9, when viewed together with these powers of intervention? In this regard, it is apparent that intervention powers elevate the relative importance of environmental outcomes in that the coastal State's rights of intervention would trump the private aspects of the Convention in conflict with such rights. It is also unlikely that the absence of Article 9 would have made any difference except for the fact that one might have had less of a problem balancing it with what appears to be contradictory outcomes in Article 5(2). While Article 9 suggests the primacy of environmental outcomes to any of the private rights under the Convention, one has Article 5(2), which seeks to reserve the rights of salvors granted under the Convention when under the control of public authorities.

Where operations are under the control of public authorities, this would typically be a function of the coastal State exercising rights in accordance with 'generally recognized principles of international law to protect its coastline'. In this regard, therefore, it is difficult to see how salvors carrying out operations under the control of public authorities may 'avail themselves of the rights and remedies ... in th[e] Convention' while these very rights are potentially threatened by States' 'measures in accordance with generally recognized principles of international law'.

One must therefore question the pasting of this public provision that confirms existing law, while also potentially resulting in the mentioned contradiction. While Article 9 clearly expresses underlying environmental protection values, its inclusion is by no means self-explanatory in relation to salvage operations except to confirm the extent of coastal States' powers. Moreover, while Article 9 adds to the idea of environmental protection as an outcome of salvage operations, it is difficult to see how it is to interact with provisions such as Articles 1(a), 8, and 14 where the environment, as mentioned, is positioned as subsidiary to property salvage outcomes.

68 Ibid s 137(1).

Article 6

Article 6 of the Convention allows for the Convention to be supplanted by a contract between the salvor and the recipient of salvage services.[69] Nevertheless, it seeks to aid environmental primacy by imposing limitations on the extent to which such contracts may impact environmental duties under the Convention. In this regard, it precludes contracts that might affect 'duties to prevent or minimize damage to the environment'.[70] Of course, as mentioned earlier in the discussion of Article 8 of the Convention, there are no independent duties in relation to the protection of the environment except to the extent that property owners may derive benefits. As such, the reference to 'duties to prevent or minimize' is simply a reference to the wording employed in Article 8 rather than an express acknowledgement of separate environmental protection duties. Rather than being a direct reference to possible environmental duties, the article seems more aimed at elevating environmental protection aims, as an expression of public policy, relative to the traditional aims of salvage, without adding to the substance of the traditional law of salvage.

Article 11

This article essentially implores coastal States, when 'regulating or deciding upon matters relating to salvage operations', to consider that the co-operation of 'salvors, other interested parties and public authorities' are necessary for 'saving life … property … and to [prevent] damage to the environment'. While States are implored in this manner, it is difficult to see how the provision amounts to anything more than a mere wish in relation to how States ought to respond in the event of shipping incidents. More so, should one consider incidents such as that involving the sinking of the oil tanker *MV Prestige*, when the governments of France, Spain, and Portugal all refused the stricken ship the right to dock. Ultimately the ship sank with 77,000 (seventy-seven thousand) tons of fuel on board, resulting in one of the biggest oil spills in Europe.[71] It imposes no positive duties on States, instead functioning as a cautionary backdrop to the exercise of rights that States may have to protect their coastlines, which may include the right to deny stricken ships entry to ports. However, the provision does not elevate environmental protection outcomes relative to property and commercial

---

69 Article 6(1).

70 Article 6(3).

71 https://safety4sea.com/cm-learn-from-the-past-prestige-sinking-one-of-the-worst-oil-spills-in-europe/ accessed 20 April 2022.

outcomes, instead calling for the appropriate balancing of interests and issues and for coastal States to recognise the importance of the salvor in a matrix that consists of 'salvors, other interested parties and public authorities'. This article, from an environmentalist perspective, does not represent a serious attempt to elevate environmental outcomes relative to commercial and property outcomes.

The Salvage Convention and Environmental Protection?

From the discussion of the Convention and the provisions pertaining to the environment, it is evident that the instrument, while expressive of environmental protection values, steers a course between the maintenance of the traditional law of salvage and the recognised social interest in environmental protection. In relation to the provision of financial incentives to encourage environmental services through special compensation, it is evidently directed at a situation where shipowners may incur liability. As such, any environmental benefits conferred outside the relationship between salvor and property owner are, at best, incidental to the performance of salvage operations as defined by the Convention. From a social interest theory and environmentalist perspective, the Convention does very little to elevate the environment relative to commercial outcomes, and certainly not in a manner that recognises the former as a fundamental concern of the law.

As to the law of salvage and its traditional limitations in relation to environmental protection, the Convention, as a response, represents a strained combination of provisions clearly geared towards a private law relationship and provisions that are aimed at taking account of an obvious broader social interest in the performance of salvage services. While the provisions of the Convention, private and public, are consequential upon an increased concern with environmental protection, the limitations of private salvage law are maintained.

Despite changes effected to the law of salvage, the understanding of salvage operations as a service owed specifically to the owners of specially recognised categories of property has remained intact. Without a willingness to expand on the basic definition of salvage services to include the environment or to directly recognise interests such as that of a coastal State in environmental protection, salvage law cannot elevate the broader interest in environmental protection relative to property outcomes. The addition of public law provisions reflective of this broader interest, at best, imposes limitations without adding a significant expansion to the law of salvage that would allow it to facilitate the broader social interest in the environment effectively and directly.

The insistence on maintaining the traditional understanding of salvage operations while attempting to steer a course between it and environmental protection does raise certain pertinent issues though. It is apparent that the addition of environmental protection outcomes challenges an area of law that has always involved the limited issue of the rescue of property at sea. While it is likely that the environmentalist may baulk at this apparently immutable aspect of salvage law, it is perhaps the case that the compromises and strict adherence to categories, as evidenced by the Convention, are there for a reason. While a strict adherence to categories may on some level limit rather than promote the environmental protection credentials of the law of salvage, any unnecessary tampering with clear definitions established over time and a refusal to accept the theoretical limitations of salvage law may result in legal uncertainty.

Perhaps salvage operations, as a functional component in a broader environmental protection framework, can best be integrated if one accepts the reality of the theoretical limitations of the law of salvage. The next chapter will therefore examine salvage operations as a functional component of coastal States' pollution response measures and salvors' claims for remuneration outside of the law of salvage.

Bibliography

Allen M, 'The International Convention on Salvage and LOF 1990' (1991) 22 J. Mar.L.&Com. 119

De La Rue, *Shipping and the Environment* (2nd edn, Informa 2009)

Gaskell, 'The 1989 Salvage Convention and the Lloyd's Open Form (LOF) Salvage Agreement 1990' (1991–1992) 16 Tul. Mar. L.J. 1, 63

Gold E, 'Marine Salvage: Towards a New Regime' (1989) 20 J.Mar.L.&Com 487, 503

Khee-Jin Tan A, *Vessel-Source Marine Pollution: The Law and Politics of International Regulation* (Cambridge OUP 2006) 38.

Liang C, 'Recent Developments in the Law of Salvage of the Marine Environment' (2001) 16 Int'l J. Marine & Coastal L. 686.

Reeder J, *Brice on the Maritime Law of Salvage* (5th edn, Sweet & Maxwell 2011)

Reeder J, *Brice on Maritime Salvage* (4th edn, Sweet & Maxwell 2003)

Rose, *Kennedy and Rose on Salvage* (7th edn, Thomson Reuters (Legal) Limited 2010)

The Travaux Préparatoires of the Convention on Salvage 1989, *Comité Maritime International*, <http://www.comitemaritime.org/Travaux-Pr%C3%A9paratoires/0,27126,112632,00.html>

Witte A, LOF and Defence of the Marine Environment <https://www.marine-salvage.com   /media-information/conference-papers/isus-associate-members-day-april-2008/>

5 Salvage Operations within Coastal State Marine Environmental Protection Measures and Salvors' Environmental Services under international instruments outside of the Law of Salvage

States' pollution response mechanisms typically recognise salvage operations and salvage capacity as integral components.[1] In this regard, at a practical level, Tsavliris has noted that 'it is only commercial salvors [that] have the equipment and expertise to prevent environmental catastrophe'.[2] This reality, of course, is also recognised in the Salvage Convention, which acknowledges the role of salvors in the protection of the environment.[3] Nevertheless, the United Kingdom's efforts to respond to marine pollution from ships precede the advent of the Salvage Convention, emanating as they do from a review by Lord Donaldson of Tymington into the powers of State intervention and command and control in salvage operations.[4]

Lord Donaldson's Review followed *The Sea Empress* incident in February 1996, in which a single-hull oil tanker ran aground off the coast of Wales with 131,000 tonnes of North Sea crude oil aboard. This review, in relation to major incidents,[5] identified salvage as one of 'four main tasks that may be associated with marine pollution incidents',[6] the others being search and rescue, clean-up at sea, and clean-up of the shoreline. As such,

---

1 See discussion of Article 11 of the Salvage Convention above, Ch 4, 67.
2 Tsavliris A, 'Pollution Prevention and Unfair Treatment of Contractors' www.marine-sal-vage.com/media-information/articles/recent/pollution-prevention-and-unfair-treatment-of-contractors/ accessed 20 March 2022.
3 See discussion of the preamble of the Salvage Convention in Chapter 4, 42.
4 Command and Control: Report of Lord Donaldson's Review of Salvage and Intervention and Their Command and Control www.publicinformationonline.com/download/90069 accessed 24 September 2021. This review was reported in 1999.
5 Ibid 45.
6 Ibid 45.

DOI: 10.4324/9781003315506-6

the review positioned salvage operations as an integral aspect of a broader framework of laws that, unlike salvage law, were primarily directed at environmental outcomes. This framework included international instruments such as the International Convention on Civil Liability for Oil Pollution Damage (the CLC) and the IOPC Fund Conventions.[7] The report envisaged a close relationship between these instruments and the 1989 Salvage Convention, basically calling for the latter's recognition of the importance of salvage operations in the context of preventive measures taken against marine pollution. In this regard the Report[8] highlighted the fact that salvage operations cannot be considered in isolation from other measures 'designed to limit the effects when ... an escape [of oil from ships] does occur'.[9] These measures include

> the aerial spraying of dispersing agents, containment by booming, at-sea recovery and shoreline clean-up. The reason for this is that while such measures are not part of the salvage operation, those controlling the salvage operation itself have to take account, so far as is possible, of the need to facilitate the deployment of these second line defences against pollution.[10]

This view of salvage as the first line of defence[11] or preventive exercise followed by 'second line defences against pollution' recognises the inherent environmental utility of property salvage operations that must ultimately complement efforts following an actual escape of oil.

The report also urged for more use of powers of intervention by the United Kingdom in marine salvage operations where ships and their cargo threatened the environment. It regarded intervention and control by the coastal State as essential in a matrix of mechanisms directed at the threat of marine pollution, which included salvage operations. This much is also

---

7 See discussion below 81 ff. See also Plant G, '"Safer Ships, Cleaner Seas": Lord Donaldson's Inquiry, the UK Government's Response and International Law' (1995) 44 *The International and Comparative Law Quarterly* 939–948. The author notes the fact that a key consequence of this report was that it influenced the United Kingdom's decision to ratify the 1989 Salvage Convention and the 1992 protocols to the 1969 International Convention on Civil Liability for Oil Pollution Damage (1969 CLC) and the 1971 Convention on the Establishment of an International Fund for Compensation for Oil Pollution Damage.

8 See above (n 4).

9 Ibid 3.

10 Ibid 3.

11 See De La Rue C and Anderson C, *Shipping and the Environment* (2nd edn, Informa, 2009) 535.

recognised in the Salvage Convention[12] although the key concern of the Convention is to maintain salvors' right to an award despite the intrusion from interests extraneous to the legal relationship between salvors and salved interests.[13]

Consequently, this chapter examines the integration of salvage capabilities in coastal States' marine environmental response plans. It also examines the extent to which salvage law complements or detracts from select instruments outside of the law of salvage that forms part of a broader matrix of environmental laws and that potentially provide alternative avenues of remuneration for salvors. The first part of the chapter looks in more detail at the recognition of salvage capability within coastal State pollution response mechanisms and the mechanisms employed to integrate such services. In this regard, the focus will be on the United Kingdom, a signatory State to the Civil Liability and Fund Conventions. For the sake of completeness and to illustrate the universal acknowledgement of salvage capability within pollution response mechanisms and mechanisms of integration, reference will also be made to the United States, which has enacted its own legislation in the form of the Oil Pollution Act 1990, instead of being party to the Civil Liability and Fund Convention scheme. The chapter does not seek to provide a complete overview of environmental protection measures but to assess the importance and positioning of salvage operations within this broader system.

The second part of the chapter examines salvors' claims under the CLC and Fund Conventions to ascertain the extent to which salvage operations and indeed salvors feature under these instruments outside of the law of salvage. More recent instruments such as the HNS Convention and the Bunker Pollution Convention of 2001 will not be discussed, although one will be able, *mutatis mutandis*, to extend the primary findings in relation to the CLC and Fund Conventions to these later instruments. This section will demonstrate how the property bias of salvage law detracts from the effective integration of salvage services into a broader environmental protection framework resulting in the unnecessary fragmentation of remuneration possibilities between two areas of law potentially applicable to environmental services within salvage operations.

12 See discussion of Articles 5 and 9 of the Salvage Convention above, Ch 4.
13 Ibid.

Salvage within Government Responses to Marine Pollution from Ships

United Kingdom

The United Kingdom implemented aspects of Lord Donaldson's Review,[14] in its National Contingency Plan for Pollution from Shipping and Offshore Installations (the NCP) in the year 2000.[15] The legal basis for this NCP was the International Convention on Oil Pollution Preparedness, Response and Co-operation 1990 (the OPRC Convention) adopted by the International Maritime Organisation (IMO) in 1990.[16] The OPRC Convention requires ships to have an 'oil pollution emergency plan' setting out reporting procedures in the event of an incident giving rise to oil pollution and the establishment of a response system to oil pollution incidents that includes a national contingency plan.[17] The UK NCP was prepared by the Secretary of State exercising a function as provided for in the Merchant Shipping Act 1995,[18] namely, 'the preparation, review and implementation of a national plan setting out arrangements for responding to incidents, which may cause marine pollution'.[19]

The NCP, in line with the Donaldson Review, is based on four aspects of intervention, namely, search and rescue, the coordination and direction of salvage operations, clean-up operations at sea, and shoreline clean-up activities.[20] It confirms the role of salvors and the need for overall control

---

14 See above (n 14).

15 In this regard, in a response to a question directed at the Secretary of State for Transport on 20 January 2003 about the last review of the United Kingdom's coastal waters counter pollution practices, it was noted that the 'National Contingency Plan for Marine Pollution from Shipping and Offshore Installations' was published in January 2000 by the Maritime and Coastguard Agency (MCA), 'following the experiences gained during [the] SEA EMPRESS incident and from the recommendations in Lord Donaldson's Review of salvage and intervention and their command and control'. See publications and records of the UK Parliament at https://publications.parliament.uk/pa/cm200203/cmhansrd/vo030120/text/30120w10.htm accessed, 19 February 2022. This represented an update of earlier NCPs, the first of which were published in 1968 in response to the *Torrey Canyon* disaster. The first solely electronic version was published in 2014 and last updated on 17 August 2017. This latest version can be accessed at www.gov.uk/government/publications/national-contingency-plannccp accessed, 19 February 2022.

16 Lord Donaldson's Review (n 249) 12 and OPRC Article 7. Also see Baughen S, 'Maritime Pollution and State Liability' in *Pollution at Sea: Law and Liability* (Informa 2012), ch 13. Accessible at www.i-law.com/ilaw/doc/view.htm?id=316091 accessed 14 March 2022.

17 OPRC Articles 3, 4, 5, and 6.

18 Merchant Shipping Act 1995.

19 Ibid s 293(2)(za).

20 Baughen S, 'Maritime Pollution and State Liability' in *Pollution at Sea* (n 16).

by the Secretary of State's Representative (SOSREP) in salvage operations where there is a threat of pollution. In terms of control it provides that '[t]he SOSREP has the ultimate and decisive voice for maritime salvage, offshore containment and intervention'.[21] Even where the SOSREP does not take control of operations or issues no directions, the NCP provides that 'salvors operate by agreement with, or with the tacit approval of the SOSREP'.[22] In this manner, the social interest in environmental protection is positioned as primary to any potential private commercial interests, which is consistent with a perspective predicated upon the environment as a fundamental concern.[23] Therefore, the difficulties noted in relation to the balancing of environmental outcomes with the property and commercial outcomes in the Salvage Convention are absent in the public law sphere, given the clarity about the precise interest, environmental protection, being pursued.

Regarding the role of salvors in the network of parties involved in pollution response measures, the NCP provides that 'incidents will be handled ... through the combined efforts of harbour masters, salvors, ship owners and crew, and MCA staff'.[24] Despite earlier indications of the central role played by salvors, they are positioned as one component of a system that involves private and public role-players. Their role is expressly subjected to the oversight powers of the SOSREP who has to 'decide whether the salvor has the capability to carry out the necessary salvage actions, in terms of experience, personnel, and material'.[25]

Therefore, the question of salvage services where the environment is threatened is no longer an issue for property owners and salvors but a function of public interest in which the environment is elevated to a primary concern. The private rights of salvors, to the extent that these may inform broader commercial interests, are essentially relegated and subsumed under the broader social interest in environmental protection. This is evidently different to the balancing difficulties noted in relation to the Salvage Convention, and accepting environmental protection as a fundamental concern is to be preferred.

The United Kingdom NCP, to the extent that it facilitates the practical involvement of salvors in pollution response measures, also reflects international sentiments expressed in the Diplomatic Conference leading up to the OPRC. The conference adopted certain resolutions to further the aims of the

---

21 NCP para 5.5.2, 11.
22 NCP para 17.7. See also s 137 of the Merchant Shipping Act 1995.
23 See discussion in Chapter 1.
24 Ibid para 17.1, 43.
25 Ibid para 17.5.

Convention,[26] some of which were of direct relevance to the position of salvors and salvage services. One of the resolutions specifically related to the 'improving [of] salvage services and recognising the essential role of salvors in response to casualties causing or likely to cause marine pollution'.[27] Moreover, in furtherance of the recognition of the role of salvors in marine pollution prevention, Resolution 8 of the Conference essentially enjoined States to 'ratify or accede to the [London Salvage Convention 1989] as soon as possible' as well as 'review the salvage capacity available to them'.[28]

This push to get States to ratify or accede to the Salvage Convention was likely predicated upon the assumption of the Convention's environmental protection credibility and the adequacy of mechanisms to encourage salvors to involve themselves in casualties representing a threat to the environment.[29] However, this vote of confidence in the Convention's ability to effectively promote the broader social interest in the environment might have been misplaced. Especially if one considers the matter from the perspective that environmental protection ought to be of fundamental concern. Nevertheless, the key roles of salvors and salvage operations in pollution response mechanisms are confirmed. Next, we will look at the contractual integration of salvage operations into pollution response measures.

Contracting for Environmental Services

United Kingdom

The primary mechanism employed to integrate salvage services into pollution response mechanisms appears to be via contract. In this regard, the United Kingdom Maritime and Coastguard Agency (MCA) can and does contract with commercial salvors.[30] As part of its remit relating to pollution response and salvage, the MCA has also devised a standard contract, the Coastguard Agreement for Salvage and Towage (CAST) to ensure that salvage and/or towage capability would be available in incidents threatening

---

26 See De La Rue and Anderson (n 11) 921ff.

27 Reeder J, *Brice on the Maritime Law of Salvage* (5th edn, Sweet & Maxwell, 2011) 463.

28 Ibid.

29 See discussion of Articles 13, 14, and 8 of the Salvage Convention in the preceding chapter.

30 A good example was the UK MCA and Ardent (salvors) agreement with the latter providing emergency towage and salvage services off the north and north-western coasts of Scotland. www.marinelog.com/shipping/salvage/ardent-signs-emergency-towage-agreement-with -uks-/ accessed 13 December 2021.

pollution. This agreement allows for a possible two-tier system of contracting by the owner of the tug in that the

> [t]owing vessel owner may as its option, obtain from the owner of any vessel or craft, which a towing vessel may be directed by the MCA to assist, a separate contract for towage and/or salvage in substitution for the hiring of that towing vessel by the MCA.[31]

As such, the tug owner appears to have the option of performing operations on the basis of the CAST contract or to enter into a separate contractual arrangement (salvage or towage) with the owner of the 'casualty vessel', which is the term used in the CAST agreement.

While, practically, this mechanism allows for commercial salvage, the CAST is evidently primarily premised upon the unavailability of ordinary commercial salvage options and the maintenance of pollution response capabilities on the part of the MCA. Nevertheless, salvage services by the towing vessel owner will either be at the request of the MCA on the terms of the CAST agreement or on the separate agreement between the towing vessel owner and the owners of the casualty vessel. Where the latter scenario unfolds, the towing vessel owner, for all intents and purposes, essentially becomes an ordinary commercial salvor.

This arrangement raises questions about the 'either or approach' in relation to legal regulatory aspects of operations under the CAST. In the event of a separate salvage contract, the towing vessel owner would presumably be remunerated on the basis of salvage law in accordance with duties as between the salvor and property owners, while the CAST establishes a contractual relationship between the towing vessel owner (salvor) and the MCA, which is primarily geared towards environmental protection.[32] In this regard, the CAST provides that

> Where a salvage contract has been entered into between the Tugowner and the Owner of any vessel or other subject of salvage, the amount recovered by the Tugowner shall remain their property and no part of the amount shall be due or payable to the MCA.[33]

---

31 Clause 6.3 of the current CAST agreement (last reviewed in 2020 and next to be reviewed in December of 2022).
32 Clause 5.1 of the CAST agreement describes 'the primary, although not exclusive, role of any towing vessel contracted' as 'emergency towage services to prevent pollution of the waters within the United Kingdom Exclusive Economic Zone and of the coastline of the United Kingdom'.
33 Ibid clause 8.1.

While the MCA's primary, although not exclusive, interest appears to be environmental protection, the right to substitute a salvage contract for the CAST suggests an assumption that the commercial salvage arrangement can effectively address environmental protection concerns. In this regard, the oversight powers of the SOSREP would certainly preclude any possibility of pollution prevention not being furthered, given its powers to direct such salvage operations. Therefore, the coastal State will receive benefits, while the responsibility for the payment of an award or any remuneration is essentially shifted to the owner of the casualty vessel. While this addresses the remunerative aspect of things from the commercial salvor's perspective, it does not address the question of benefits conferred that exceed the extent of the property owner's liabilities.

However, the towing vessel owner may also perform environmental services without entering into a separate salvage agreement with the owners of the casualty vessel. In such a case, the CAST agreement and the payment mechanism provided thereunder will remain intact. In this regard clause 8.2 of the CAST provides for the situation where no separate salvage contract has been entered into, where 'the towing vessel owner may, if it appears reasonable and practicable to do so, claim salvage from the subject being salved without prejudice to this [the CAST] Agreement and their right to receive hire [in terms of CAST].' This allows for the possibility that the salvor might be remunerated on a more lucrative basis in that hire payable under the CAST agreement would remain payable together with the entitlement to a salvage award.

However, clause 8.3 of the CAST removes the possibility of the towing vessel owner being paid hire together with a separate salvage award or other remuneration. The towing vessel owner [salvor] is required to 'reimburse the MCA for hire paid to the towing vessel owner during the period of the salvage services'. This mechanism implies that the salvor, while engaged in the salvage operation is not acting in terms of the CAST or bestowing the benefit that is contemplated under CAST, despite CAST remaining intact. Essentially, the salvor has a choice of a salvage award with CAST potentially functioning as a deductible so to speak in that monies paid under the CAST hire will have to be reimbursed.

While the CAST arrangement clearly recognises the importance of the availability of salvage capability in the prevention of pollution, it treats the commercial salvage arrangement between the tug owner and the owner of salved property as suspending the former in relation to the remuneration of the salvor. At the same time, the salvors' services under the CAST are primarily although not exclusively 'that of ... services to prevent pollution of the waters within the United Kingdom Exclusive Economic Zone (UK

EEZ) and of the coastline of the United Kingdom'.[34] This suggests that salvors' attempt to obtain a salvage award is not a service to prevent pollution and hence, that the MCA is to be reimbursed. It essentially denies the extent to which salvage law itself has an environmental protection outcome, even if not sufficiently promoted relative to private rights, or that the operations are still achieving the aims of the CAST agreement.

Essentially, the MCA continues to receive the benefit of environmental protection in the sense that the very rescue of property may also prevent pollution, although this is now subsumed under the law of salvage. So, while the benefit of pollution prevention is conferred, the conclusion of a separate commercial salvage arrangement simply shifts the responsibility for payment to the owner of the salved property as a concern of the law of salvage.[35] Essentially a salvor will have to engage in careful calculations to ascertain whether they wish to claim a salvage award or proceed on the basis of the CAST and hire payable thereunder. This is an untenable situation, due to the nature of emergency salvage operations, as they do not lend themselves the luxury of time to make appropriate commercial decisions. Such a cost–benefit analysis at a time when prompt action is needed could only undermine the importance of environmental protection as a fundamental concern in salvage operations.

United States of America

The United States is not a party to the International Convention on Civil Liability for Oil Pollution Damage and has enacted its own comprehensive legislation to deal with oil spill compensation and liability in the form of the Oil Pollution Act 1990 (OPA).[36] With the OPA, the United States Congress consolidated existing federal oil spill laws under one programme.[37] The OPA was also the United States' attempt to expand its own NCP.[38] As such, the

---

34 Clause 5.1.
35 Article 14 of the Salvage Convention.
36 The Oil Pollution Act of 1990 (33 U.S.C. 2701–2761).
37 Ramseur J, *Oil Spill in U.S. Coastal Waters: Background, Governance, and Issues for Congress* (Diane Publishing, 2010) 9.
38 The United States' National Contingency Plan was developed and first published in 1968 making it the first comprehensive system of accident reporting, spill containment, and clean-up. The original plan also established a response headquarters, a national reaction team, and regional reaction teams, essentially pre-empting the later and current National Response Team and Regional Response Teams (information sourced from www.epa.gov /emergency-response/national-oil-and-hazardous-substances-pollution-contingency-plan -ncp-overview accessed 14 December 2021.

United States' NCP reflects the oil spill provisions of the OPA,[39] providing for a 'multi-layered planning and response system to improve preparedness and response to spills in marine environments'.[40] The OPA, similar to the situation in the United Kingdom, also places salvors within the framework of efforts directed at the prevention of pollution from ships.

The OPA requires the development of a Vessel Response Plan (VRP) to minimise the impact of oil spills.[41] These VRPs are administered by the United States Coast Guard (USCG), the designated lead response agency in relation to oil spills in coastal waters.[42] It is within the context of these VRPs that the integral role played by salvors in pollution prevention and response measures is highlighted. For example, in relation to non-tanker vessels, owners of such vessels with an oil-carrying capacity of 2500 barrels or greater are required to pre-contract with, amongst other, salvors.[43] The need for this requirement has been expressed as follows:

> This pre-planning will create vital linkages between the shipping industry and oil spill response service providers (such as oil spill removal organizations (OSROs), *salvage companies*, and marine firefighting companies), ensuring that mechanisms are in place to immediately respond to an emergency.[44]

Again, there is a clear recognition of the role of salvors in emergency pollution response mechanisms, while the idea of 'vital linkages' alludes to the importance of proper collaboration between the different role-players. Therefore, under the US system, pre-existing salvage arrangements are a component in a network of measures directed at the prevention of pollution. This appears to be a clear recognition of the preventative aspect of property salvage operations relative to environmental outcomes, the former having been described as the 'principal tool for prevention'.[45]

39 See the 'National Oil and Hazardous Substances Pollution Contingency Plan (NCP) Overview' www.epa.gov/emergency-response/national-oil-and-hazardous-substances-pollution-contingency-plan-ncp-overview accessed 15 December 2021.
40 Ramsuer J (n 37).
41 (n 36). Sec 5006.
42 Oil Spills Prevention and Preparedness Regulations www.epa.gov/oil-spills-prevention-and-preparedness-regulations accessed 14 December 2021.
43 UK P&I Club Circular, October 2013, Ref14/13.
44 Federal Register 2013, Vol 78 No 189 www.ukpandi.com/fileadmin/uploads/uk-pi/Documents/Environmental/GMS%20Client%20Advisory%2015-13%20-%20NTVRP%20Final%20Rule%20Attachment.pdf (emphasis added).
45 Marine Salvage: 'A Closer Look at OPA 90's Success' www.americansalvage.org/marine-log/ML-Mar2014.pdf accessed 14 December 2021.

The DONJON-SMIT VRP salvage pre-arrangement provides an example of a contract entered into between the provider of salvage and lighter services and a shipowner.[46] This contract is not a salvage contract, but a contract providing for the 'provision of and access to salvage, firefighting and lightering services for OWNER's vessels trading in U.S. waters as and when required'.[47] As such, the agreement is essentially a framework arrangement in terms of which the contractor may provide salvage, towage, or wreck-removal services. The contract makes provision for three categories of services ranging from category one, which only requires towage services, to category three situations where proper salvage operations might be required.[48] Such a category three situation might be a matter of pure property salvage or one that includes a 'threat of damage to the environment within the meaning of Article 14 of the Salvage Convention of 1989'.[49]

Unlike the United Kingdom CAST agreement, the DONJON-SMIT agreement is not exclusively directed at environmental protection, given that it provides for 'pollution control/containment/abatement',[50] as an 'either or' possibility, essentially contemplating the possibility of pure pollution control/containment/abatement services. Nevertheless, where salvage services are performed, with or without an environmental protection dimension, these will be based on the Lloyd's Open Form 2011[51] in the form as attached as an annex to the agreement 'without amendment'.[52]

Essentially, the agreement allows for the provision of services based on already existing industry standard contracts, with the ultimate choice of contract dependent on the services required. Essentially, the legal position of salvors relative to shipowners, in line with the law of salvage, will remain the same. The legal relationship will be between the shipowner and DONJON-SMIT, with the limitations this brings about in relation to the interests of the coastal State and the remuneration of salvors. This is essentially the result of the contractual relationship continuing to exist as between the private commercial parties, namely DONJON_SMIT and the owners of property.

---

46 DONJON-SMIT, LLC Oil Pollution Act of 1990 Salvage, Firefighting and Lightering Contract and Funding Agreement www.ukpandi.com/media/files/imports/13108/wordings /11158-donjonsmit-tank-and-nontank-version-a-october-4-201.pdf accessed 26 August 2022.

47 Ibid. Recitals of the contract.

48 Ibid. Article 2, definitions section.

49 Ibid.

50 Ibid. Article 3(d).

51 Ibid. Article 6(a)(iii).

52 Ibid.

The key difference between the DONJON-SMIT and CAST agreement is the latter's establishing of a direct contractual relationship between the salvor and the United Kingdom's MCA, which amounts to a more direct furthering of the social interest in environmental protection. This, as will be shown in the next part of the chapter, is the key to any approach that seeks to reduce the problem of fragmentation and to allow for a law of salvage that complements rather than detracts from a broader legal framework directed at the protection of the environment. Nevertheless, while the nature of the contracts may differ, the CAST and DONJON-SMIT contracts are a clear recognition of the utility value of contract to integrate private commercial salvors into the broader matrix of laws geared towards pollution response.

While a coastal State such as the United Kingdom may be willing to incur costs to keep tugs in a state of readiness, the payment of remuneration where salvors are engaged in salvage operations is simply shifted to the owner of the ship as a concern of salvage law proper with the consequences and limitations that entail. The focus, therefore, still appears to be the liability of salved property owners rather than the service rendered to the coastal State. This reluctance on the part of coastal States to detach the question of property salvage and rights thereunder from the environmental service rendered by salvors means that the limitations noted in relation to the payment of awards for such services remain.[53] Moreover, as shown in the next section dealing with remuneration possibilities outside of salvage, this also detracts from these possibilities, which results in unnecessary fragmentation and a law of salvage that does not complement a broader environmental law framework. So, while these contracts between coastal States via the agency of the relevant authorities and private commercial interests show a definite positive development in the practical integration of salvage services into environmental protection, they still operate on the understanding of the law of salvage as the ultimate regulatory framework for remuneration of environmental services.

Instruments of Remuneration outside of Salvage

Salvors can potentially claim remuneration for environmental services under certain international instruments outside of the law of salvage. These opportunities are available under the 1992 International Convention on Civil Liability for Oil Pollution Damage (the CLC) and the 1992 Fund Conventions. In this regard, the CLC, in connection with claims for pollution damage, expressly includes, under pollution damage, 'the costs

---

53 See discussion of Articles 13 and 14 above, Ch 4. 45 ff.

of preventive measures and further loss or damage caused by preventive measures'.[54] Additionally, it also provides in Article 1(7) that '"Preventive measures" means any reasonable measures taken by any person [potentially a salvor] after an incident has occurred to prevent or minimize pollution damage'.

Nevertheless, as will be shown, the maintenance of traditional notions of salvage under the Salvage Convention creates difficulties for salvors seeking to avail themselves of these remuneration opportunities. The extent to which these liability and compensation instruments interact with the Salvage Convention will also shed light on the manner in which the law of salvage ought to serve a broader marine environmental protection network that is more than an indirect recognition of the utility value of salvage but is actually reflected in a sound legal theoretical manner. However, before examining the possibility of claims by salvors under these instruments, a brief description of these instruments will be given.

1992 International Convention on Civil Liability for Oil Pollution Damage (CLC) and 1992 Fund Convention

Four Conventions have operated in the international system of compensation for oil pollution from ships.[55] These conventions are the Civil Liability Convention (CLC) 1969, establishing the tanker owners' liability for pollution damage, the Fund Convention (FC) 1971 providing supplementary compensation; and the CLC 1992 and FC 1992, which are revised versions of the initial CLC and FC.[56] The CLC (1969 and 1992),[57] and the Fund, together, provide a tiered approach to the economic compensation for oil spill damage.[58] Essentially, the 1992 Fund Convention, supplementary to the 1992 CLC, compensates victims in the situation where compensation under the 1992 CLC is not available or is considered to be inadequate. Under the 1992 CLC Convention, the shipowner or the shipowner's Protection & Indemnity Club (P&I Club) is liable to provide the first tier of

---

54 CLC Art 1(6)(b). The more recent HNS and Bunker Pollution Convention provide for the same in their respective definitions of damage.

55 Chao Wu, 'Liability and Compensation for Oil Pollution Damage: Some Current Threats to the International Convention System' (2002) 7 *Spill Science & Technology Bulletin* 105–112.

56 Ibid.

57 The CLC 1992 operates in most States party to the CLC system and it provides for higher compensation limits. See also De La Rue and Anderson (n 11) 137.

58 See Mason M, 'Civil Liability for Oil Pollution Damage: Examining the Evolving Scope for Environmental Compensation in the International Regime' (2003) 27 *Marine Policy* 1.

compensation. A second tier of compensation is provided under the Fund Convention, if the compensation available under the CLC is inadequate from the International Oil Pollution Compensation Fund (IOPC) provided. The IOPC Fund is made up, largely, of levies made on oil companies.[59] In this manner it is apparent that, unlike the situation of special compensation under the Salvage Convention, cargo owners in the form of the oil industry are more involved in efforts directed at environmental protection. This allows for the fairer spread of costs over the relevant commercial sectors. Being supplementary to the CLC, the fund pays out an amount less the amount paid by the shipowner for damage incurred by Governments, local authorities, companies, and private citizens because of oil spills.[60]

CLC 1992

The 1992 Civil Liability Convention governs the liability of shipowners for oil pollution damage.[61] It provides for strict liability for shipowners, except where they can show that pollution damage resulted from acts of war or irresistible natural phenomena,[62] the intentional acts of third parties,[63] or the negligent or other wrongful acts of any government or public authority.[64] The shipowner is also entitled to limit his liability to an amount that is linked to the tonnage of his ship,[65] save where the shipowner causes pollution intentionally or recklessly and with the knowledge that such damage would probably result.[66]

International Oil Pollution Compensation (IOPC) Funds

The IOPC Funds are two intergovernmental organisations (the 1992 Fund and the Supplementary Fund) that provide compensation for oil pollution

---

59   In proportion to the tonnage of oil they receive.

60   A third tier of compensation is also available in some countries that have ratified the Protocol of 2003 to The International Convention on the Establishment of an International Fund for Compensation for Oil Pollution Damage, 1992. Article 4(1) of the Protocol provides that '[t]he Supplementary Fund shall pay compensation to any person suffering pollution damage if such person has been unable to obtain full and adequate compensation for an established claim for such damage under the terms of the 1992 Fund Convention'. See also De La Rue and Anderson (n 11) 82.

61   CLC Article III(1).

62   Article III(2)(a).

63   Article III(2)(b).

64   Article III(2)(c).

65   CLC Article V.

66   CLC Article V(2).

damage that occurs in Member States, resulting from spills of persistent oil from tankers.[67] As mentioned earlier, the limited compensation available under the CLC and the need for this to be increased gave rise to the 1992 CLC and the 1993 Fund Convention.[68] In the wake of the *Erika* and *Prestige* incidents, a supplementary Fund Protocol was adopted in 2003, which provided for compensation over and above that of the 1992 Fund Convention, in States that are parties to the Protocol.[69] These IOPC Funds are funded by contributions paid by recipients of certain types of oil by sea transport, with contributions based on the volume of oil received in a relevant calendar year. In this way, the oil industry itself is taking some responsibility in relation to pollution damage. This is not reflected in the way the Salvage Convention allows for special compensation paid to salvors except for the extent to which cargo interests might contribute to an Article 13 award where presumably the 'skill and efforts of the salvors in preventing or minimizing damage to the environment'[70] have been considered. As such, unlike special compensation under the Salvage Convention, the IOPC's fund allows for a bigger compensatory pool as well as a more equitable spread of costs over the relevant industries.

Salvors under the CLC and Fund Conventions

A salvor who has performed environmental services could potentially recover compensation under the CLC. A salvor might be interested in pursuing this avenue in the event of his inability to enforce a claim for special compensation under Article 14 of the Convention.[71] As noted already, Article I(7) of the CLC provides for the costs of 'preventative' measures to be recovered defining this as 'any reasonable measures taken by any person after an incident has occurred to prevent or minimize pollution damage'. Nevertheless, given the definition of 'pollution damage', as 'loss or damage caused outside the ship by contamination resulting from the escape or discharge of oil from the ship',[72] a salvor seeking to claim would probably have to show that services went beyond those of an ordinary salvage operation.

On a reading of Article 8 of the Salvage Convention, there appears to be a conflict between services meeting the requirement under the Salvage

---

67 www.iopcfunds.org/about-us/ last accessed 11 January 2022.
68 Ibid.
69 Ibid.
70 1989 Salvage Convention Article 13(1)(b). See discussion in Chapter 4.
71 See De La Rue and Anderson (n 11) 588.
72 CLC Article 1(6)(a).

Convention and those under the CLC. In relation to environmental services regulated under the former, the salvor's environmental services are expressed with reference to the performance of the actual salvage operation. Under the CLC, environmental services to prevent pollution damage, as defined under the instrument, presupposes a degree of failure in the property salvage operation. This creates a tension between the salvor's private law duties under the Convention and the pursuing of a claim under the CLC, which would entail services beyond those rendered to the property owners.

Difficulties Created by the Salvage Convention for Claims under the CLC

As will be shown, definitions employed within the law of salvage, as well as the secondary nature of environmental protection, create potential difficulties for salvors' claims under the CLC. These difficulties primarily relate to the purpose that informs salvage operations as well as the assessment of costs that a salvor could recover.[73]

Purpose of Preventative Measures and Salvage

The CLC allows reasonable measures taken by 'any person',[74] but only where measures taken in the preventing or minimising of pollution damage were specifically directed at this outcome. As explained in the previous chapter, environmental services in salvage operations are incidental to property salvage operations and merely a factor in the determination of properly performed property salvage operations. Therefore, one might question whether a salvor's actions were directed at pollution prevention, as required under the CLC, or the salvage of property. If it is the latter, then the salvor does not meet the requirement that its actions must have been directed at the prevention of pollution as a primary purpose. Although the Salvage Convention recognises the role of salvors in environmental protection, effectively acknowledging a dual purpose to salvage operations,[75] the clear property bias in its provisions creates difficulties for salvors, given the requirement under the CLC that the purpose of measures taken must be pollution prevention.

These difficulties are highlighted by De La Rue and Anderson in commenting on the various parties that may be involved in salvage operations where there is a threat to the environment (owners, salvors, insurers, and

---

73   See De La Rue and Anderson (n 11) 589.
74   CLC Article I(7).
75   See De La Rue and Anderson (n 11) 394.

public authorities monitoring salvage operations), and how they may attribute different priorities to outcomes.[76] Aside from duties imposed on salvors, a calculation of the value of the property at risk and the prospect of success as opposed to the extent of possible pollution and remuneration in excess of a property salvage award may inform motives.[77] Calculations might also change over the time of the salvage operation, suggesting a murky situation of changing motives and potentially divergent interests. Nevertheless, a few cases may shed light on the way these issues have been approached.

An Italian case, the *Patmos* (Italy, 1985),[78] considered whether salvage operations were covered by the definition of pollution damage under the CLC 1969 – essentially, whether salvage operations constituted preventive measures for the purpose of the CLC. The court of first instance confirmed that salvage operations were not preventive measures because salvage was primarily directed at the rescue of property, namely ship and cargo. Nevertheless, the court acknowledged that salvage operations might have the effect of preventing pollution but that this was not enough to change the primary purpose of salvage. However, it is not certain whether this conclusion was informed by an assessment of salvors' motives or the perceived legal nature of salvage as a service to property. Clear though, was that the court was not willing to attach any weight to environmental protection as an incidental outcome of salvage operations when their supposed purpose was property rescue, whether informed by salvors' motives or the legal regulatory framework.

Of course, this case was decided prior to the Salvage Convention 1989 and one can only speculate on the effect that the environmental provisions in the instruments might have had on the court's conclusion in relation to the purpose of the salvage operation. However, as discussed in the previous chapter, the statement of purpose of the Convention in its preamble is not borne out by its substantive provisions. The Convention has retained the traditional definition of salvage operations as a service to property and the court's decision is consistent with this. As such, it is likely that the court would have reached a similar conclusion.

In the *Rio Orinoco* case (Canada, 16 October 1990),[79] the question of the relationship between salvage and preventive measures, as well as the

---

76 Ibid.

77 Ibid.

78 See the Oil Pollution Compensation Fund Annual Report 1988 60, where the case is discussed.

79 See the Oil Pollution Compensation Fund Annual Report 1990 45. Accessible at www .iopcfunds.org/uploads/tx_iopcpublications/1991_ENGLISH_ANNUAL_REPORT.pdf last accessed 1 March 2022.

question of claimant's motives under the CLC, also arose.[80] The court considered attempts to remove the *Rio Orinoco* and her cargo to be within the definitions of 'pollution damage' and 'preventive measures' provided in Articles I(6) and I(7) of the CLC because the primary purpose of these operations was to prevent pollution.[81] Interestingly also, the Fund accepted that these operations, during certain periods, had a dual purpose – to prevent and minimise pollution and to salve the vessel and the cargo.[82] The key, however, was to distinguish between those aspects of the operation directed at pollution prevention and those directed at the saving of property. Therefore, as in the *Patmos*, it remained essential for a claim under the CLC that the primary purpose must have been to prevent or minimise pollution.

While the Fund highlighted the issue of motive, the essential difference between the *Rio Orinoco* and the *Patmos* cases was the prominent involvement of the Canadian government as a claimant in the former. Essentially, while the relationship between salvage and preventive measures under the CLC was an issue, the motive of the salvors was subsumed under that of the coastal authority (acting for the Canadian government), and it was the latter's motive that became relevant. As noted by De La Rue and Anderson,[83] 'the active involvement of the Canadian Government, and its controlling influence over the operations, left no room for doubt that pollution avoidance was the overriding purpose'. This makes sense in that the purpose for the involvement of commercial salvors by coastal States is pollution response capability. In their exercise of control over salvage operations, the primary purpose is to ensure that the environment is not placed at risk by commercial property salvage operations. As such, any claim by such a coastal State would be premised upon the idea of recovering costs incurred for measures intended to 'prevent or minimize pollution damage'.[84]

According to De La Rue and Anderson, in the ascertainment of purpose in the *Patmos* and *Rio Orinoco* cases, the purpose of the claimants was clear, and it outweighed other possible purposes.[85] Nevertheless, while it would be difficult to argue against the idea that any governmental involvement is driven by environmental protection concerns, motive might not necessarily be the best basis upon which to determine entitlement to compensation under the CLC and Fund Conventions. In this regard, it has already been mentioned that motives can change during salvage operations while

---

80 Ibid 48.
81 Ibid 50.
82 ibid.
83 De La Rue and Anderson (n 11) 398.
84 CLC Article 1(7).
85 Ibid. De La Rue and Anderson (n 11) 398.

different parties might have different primary outcomes in mind. When, for example, would a shipowner's purpose be to prevent or minimise damage to the environment as opposed to minimising its own liabilities, especially given the direct relationship between these two issues? Is it enough to suggest that the mere intention to minimise liability is subsumed under the practical outcome of environmental protection to the extent that liability is indeed prevented or minimised? On a reading of Article 1(7), the answer to this last question must be no.

Evidently, an unclear purpose might result in significant difficulties in ascertaining the validity of a claim under the CLC. Added to the above complications is the possibility that costs to be recovered might have to be apportioned between different measures directed at different aspects (environmental and property) of the salvage operations.[86] In this regard, De La Rue and Anderson, referring to the *Tarpenbek* incident, suggest that instead of looking at operations as a whole, a segmental approach might be more appropriate.[87]

> where the primary purpose of an operation is to avoid pollution, a deduction may nevertheless be made for the cost of specific measures serving a different purpose, such as recovery of the wreck of the ship after the oil has been removed.

Perhaps the above example would be a situation where such a determination can be made. However, not all measures taken can be easily categorised as measures taken towards environmental protection as opposed to those exclusively directed at property salvage. This much is also admitted by the authors who have noted that this approach has its limitations in that it might be difficult to ascertain the actual purpose of a specific measure.[88] Moreover, a single measure could have a dual purpose, in that the saving of property might be necessary for the prevention or minimising of pollution.[89] As such, too much emphasis on motive or purpose might create unnecessary difficulties by ignoring the fact that decisions often have to be made quickly in difficult circumstances.

---

86 Ibid 399.
87 Ibid. The authors refer to the *Tarpenbek* incident where the 1971 fund took the position that while the primary purpose of the contract was to avoid pollution, the threat of pollution ceased when the oil was removed from the tanker and that subsequent costs were not recoverable under the CLC.
88 Ibid.
89 This also appears to be the primary value of property salvage operations within the broader network of laws aimed at environmental protection or pollution response.

While one could logically sever salvage-specific measures from operations directed primarily at pollution prevention, the converse might not necessarily be true. The fact that one directs attention to the prevention of pollution presupposes a successful property salvage operation. As such, a measure primarily directed at the rescue of property in a situation where there is a threat to the environment inevitably furthers environmental protection. However, as per the *Patmos* decision, the possibility of a recovery under the CLC is precluded as pollution prevention as a practical consequence of property salvage is not recognised as amenable to compensation under the CLC.

Nevertheless, the *Portfield* incident suggests that salvage operations that are prolonged due to environmental protection concerns may contain elements that could be compensated as preventive measures.[90] The *Portfield* sank with a cargo of diesel and medium fuel oil while at berth in Pembroke Dock, Wales,[91] and salvage operations were prolonged and more expensive because of additional efforts to prevent oil pollution.[92] De La Rue and Anderson suggest that, despite the fact that the starting point for the analysis in this case was 'that the operations had salvage as their primary purpose',[93] the shipowner, claiming compensation for preventive measures, maintained that the primary purpose of the operations was to prevent oil pollution.[94] The shipowner contended that salvage operations would have been completed within hours and at a much lower cost, but for the risk to the environment. As such, the primary purpose of the operations was the protection of the environment.

This factual finding in the *Portfield* incident distinguishes the matter from the *Patmos*, while still consistent with the idea that salvage operations primarily directed at the rescue of property but with environmental benefits would not be amenable to compensation under the CLC for preventive measures taken. Nevertheless, the former incident cannot be regarded as an instance where salvage was the primary purpose with added preventive measures. Instead, in a case like this, it would be essential for a claimant salvor to be able to show how added measures could have been omitted in the salvaging of property. Showing this would then raise the very real presumption that added measures must have been directed at something other than property salvage, namely environmental protection.

90   IOPC Fund Annual Report 1991 51.
91   Ibid.
92   Ibid.
93   De La Rue and Anderson (n 11) 400.
94   IOPC Fund Annual Report 1991 51.

However, a salvor might potentially be trumped by the way that potential 'environmental duties' are expressed in the Salvage Convention as intrinsic to properly performed salvage operations,[95] while, more generally, environmental outcomes are positioned as incidental to salvage operations. Given that the 'duty' to prevent or minimise environmental damage is imposed in so far as it is necessary to effect salvage operations, this might suggest that preventative measures were not in relation to the environment but, legally, in furtherance of property salvage operations.

Nevertheless, clean-up measures beyond the confines of the salvage operations would constitute preventive measures under the CLC. Of course, while a salvor could go beyond statutorily or even contractually defined duties to prevent or minimise environmental damage, this might constitute a breach of the duty within the law of salvage as these would not be directed, as defined under the Salvage Convention, at the proper performance of property salvage operations. Therefore, we have a tension created by competing interests (private and public) and to no small degree due to restrictive definitions employed in two areas of law that both seek to further environmental values. In this regard, the extent to which the law of salvage appears to be at odds with possible redress under the CLC is well encapsulated by the observations of Wang.[96]

> A salvage operation is an event which can precede, accompany, and follow an oil spill, and hence, is likely to constitute a complicating factor in an analysis of compensation claims.[97]

While Wang does not explain the nature of the complications posed by salvage operations, these can be attributed to the maintenance of the traditional view of salvage as a service to property under the Salvage Convention. Although the instrument acknowledges the importance of salvors and salvage operations for environmental protection, it does not elevate environmental protection as a primary or even equal outcome of salvage relative to commercial property outcomes. This, as shown, detracts from remuneration possibilities for salvors under the CLC, while also contributing to the fragmented legal treatment of environmental services and their remuneration in salvage operations.

---

95 See discussion of Article 8 of the Salvage Convention in Chapter 4.
96 Wang Hui, *Civil Liability for Marine Oil Pollution Damage: A Comparative and Economic Study of the International, US and Chinese Compensation Regime* (Energy and Environmental Law and Policy Series) (Wolters Kluwer Alphen aan den Rijn, 2011).
97 Ibid 271.

The Assessment of Costs that a Salvor May Recover

Aside from issues in relation to the purpose of actions undertaken in the context of salvage operations, the costs claimable by salvors could also prove to be problematic.[98] Essentially, recoverable costs under the CLC might be more restrictive than under Article 14 of the Salvage Convention.[99] The key issue is that the shipowner might potentially be a claimant under the CLC, where it has already paid a salvor for salvage services. In such a situation the compensation will be assessed with reference to the costs of the shipowner in relation to measures undertaken rather than the costs of the salvor.[100]

This issue is exacerbated by the fact that the costs of the shipowner are probably restricted by the way environmental services under the Salvage Convention are linked to the property salvage operation. This would explain the contention that recoverable costs of the salvor might be more restrictive. The situation would probably be the same where salvors act under the direction of coastal authorities, where the latter would likely be the claimant under the CLC as demonstrated in the *Rio Orinoco* case.

One may assume that any payment received by a salvor would be set off against a potential claim under the CLC. In this regard, De La Rue and Anderson appear to doubt the extent to which the IOPC Fund would be prepared to take into account costs over and above those immediately relevant to the operations.[101] For example, the IOPC Fund might not be as concerned with the question of the maintenance of salvage capabilities, which under the Salvage Convention influenced the idea of salvors' overhead charges also being taken into account in the payment of special compensation.[102] Nevertheless, the salvor's actions and performance of duties beyond those owed to the shipowner under the Salvage Convention ought to be recoverable under the CLC.

Concluding Remarks

This chapter demonstrated the significance of salvage operations in a broader framework of measures directed at the prevention of pollution from ships and the effectiveness of contract to integrate commercial salvors

---

98 De La Rue and Anderson (n 11) 590.
99 Ibid.
100 Ibid.
101 Ibid.
102 *Semco Salvage & Marine Pte Ltd v Lancer Navigation Co Ltd (The Nagasaki Spirit)* [1997] 1 Lloyd's Rep. 323 [HL].

into this network. In this regard both the United Kingdom and the United States, the latter with its own form of oil pollution compensation scheme, have opted for the contractual integration of salvage services into pollution response measures. In the United States' integration of salvage contracts into their VRPs, one still has the situation where the coastal State's interests are promoted but payment for receipt of this benefit is shifted to the owner of salved property as a concern of the law of salvage, with the limitations implicit to that approach.

This is different from the United Kingdom's approach, where the integration of salvage services into pollution response measures is by means of a direct contractual relationship between the MCA and the relevant salvors or tug owners. This provides for the direct remuneration of the salvor by the recipient of the benefit conferred, outside of the law of salvage. However, this is dependent on the salvor not entering into a separate salvage agreement with the owner of salved property.

Where a separate contract for towage or salvage is concluded, the CAST is terminated, with remuneration being treated as a matter of the law of salvage. In relation to remuneration possibilities under the CLC and Fund Conventions, this may create difficulties for the claimant salvor as questions regarding the intention of the salvor may arise. As such, one must question the need to view commercial salvage contracts as a substitute for the MCA Cast agreement. Keeping it intact would enable the salvor to receive payment for services rendered, while a claim by the coastal State under the CLC and Fund Conventions will not be challenged by questions of primary intentions accompanying property salvage operations.

As noted, the key problem with salvors' claims under the CLC and Fund Conventions is the fact that salvage operations are directed, primarily, at the rescue of property. This intention, as shown, will prove fatal to a claim under the CLC and Fund Conventions, although exceptions, such as where operations can be said to have a dual purpose, exist. Should the CAST agreement remain applicable, especially given the primary duty under these contracts to safeguard coastlines against pollution, this would be a clear indication that salvage operations were directed at environmental protection, with property salvage a secondary concern. However, as noted, the State will have to be the claimant as the salvor would have been remunerated for its services in terms of the contract with the coastal State. This means that the remuneration of the salvor, based as it is on the provision of environmental protection services, can be recouped by the State. There would simply be no reason for salvors to claim under these instruments with the added difficulties of having to distinguish between actions primarily directed at environmental protection and those directed at property salvage. An important consequence of this would be that the two systems of property salvage and environmental protection instruments outside of the law of salvage will be more complementary, while also taking care of the unnecessary fragmented approach to the question of salvor's remuneration for environmental services in salvage operations.

Bibliography

Baughen S, 'Maritime Pollution and State Liability' in *Pollution at Sea: Law and Liability* (Informa 2012), ch 13. <https://www.i-law.com/ilaw/doc/view.htm?id=316091>

Command and Control: Report of Lord Donaldson's Review of Salvage and Intervention and Their Command and Control <https://www.publicinformationonline.com/download/90069> accessed 24 September 2021. This review was reported in 1999

De La Rue C and Anderson C, *Shipping and the Environment* (2nd edn, Informa 2009)

Mason M, 'Civil Liability for Oil Pollution Damage: Examining the Evolving Scope for Environmental Compensation in the International Regime' (2003) 27 1 Marine Policy 1–12

Plant G, '"Safer Ships, Cleaner Seas": Lord Donaldson's Inquiry, the UK Government's Response and International Law' (1995) 44 The International and Comparative Law Quarterly 939–948

Ramseur J, *Oil Spill in U.S. Coastal Waters: Background, Governance, and Issues for Congress* (Diane Publishing 2010)

Reeder J, *Brice on the Maritime Law of Salvage* (5th edn, Sweet & Maxwell 2011)

Wang H, *Civil Liability for Marine Oil Pollution Damage: A Comparative and Economic Study of the International, US and Chinese Compensation Regime (Energy and Environmental Law and Policy Series)* (Wolters Kluwer Alphen aan den Rijn, 2011)

Wu C, 'Liability and Compensation for Oil Pollution Damage: Some Current Threats to the International Convention System' (2002) 7 Spill Science & Technology Bulletin 105–112

6 Contracts between Coastal States and Salvors as the Legal Regulatory Framework for Environmental Services in the Context of Salvage Operations

This study questioned the choice of the law of salvage as the appropriate legal regulatory framework for environmental services in salvage operations. In doing so, it was premised upon a perspective in which environmental protection values were of fundamental concern. As such, the study deviated from what appears to be the standard discourse relating to environmental protection in salvage operations, namely the introduction of fundamental changes to the law of salvage, such as the introduction of environmental awards.

Chapter 1 provided an overview of Pound's social interest theory and its application by the late Professor Barend Van Niekerk in his identification of the environment as a fundamental concern of the law. The key aspect of this social interest theory is the use of law as a tool to realise and balance preferences and demands (values). As such, this theory essentially demands that one adopts a functional approach to law in which outcomes we sought should inform the way we formulate laws and indeed categorise matters. Against the backdrop of environmental protection as a fundamental concern, the social interest theory would dictate that the law of salvage should aim to balance the broader social interests in environmental protection against the social interest in international trade. More importantly, accepting that environmental protection is a fundamental concern or norm, this needs to be achieved in a manner that is at least on an equal level with commercial concerns and complementary to broader environmental protection measures.

Chapter 2 provided an historical overview of the law of salvage. This overview, in line with Chapter 2, highlighted the extent to which the development of early salvage law was often incidental to the achievement of broader social aims. As such, specific mischiefs or the attainment of specific goals functioned as developmental triggers in early salvage law.

DOI: 10.4324/9781003315506-7

This adaptability of salvage law to address these outcomes partly explains assumptions that this system could simply be adjusted to address environmental protection outcomes. This could also be attributed to the central and well-acknowledged role of salvors as a first line of defence in the prevention or minimising of pollution. Essentially, the utility of salvage operations in marine casualties posing a threat to the environment almost pre-empted the development of an environmental dimension to salvage.

Nevertheless, as demonstrated, the environmental dimension to salvage also represents a significant departure from what was historically the core concern of salvage, namely, the rescue of property. In this regard, the historical overview has shown that the safeguarding of property was always central to developments in salvage. From an English law perspective, this was partly due to its placement within the equitable jurisdiction of the Admiralty court. The legal theoretical nature and definitions employed in salvage took shape within a commercial context, which coupled with its placement in Admiralty, resulted in a legal regulatory framework limited to services to property at sea, unconcerned with the environment.

Chapter 3 examined the legal theoretical nature of the law of salvage. From this discussion it was evident that the basis of salvage was the equity of rewarding salvors for benefits conferred upon the owners of maritime property and the policy of encouraging salvors in furtherance of marine commerce. This policy component of salvage also explains the development of liberal salvage awards for the safeguarding and rescuing of property. However, should we wish to incorporate environmental outcomes into the fabric of salvage in the same way as commercial outcomes, we will have to alter standard definitions. This is likely to introduce unnecessary uncertainty into an established area of law.

Chapter 4 provided an analysis of the Salvage Convention. The Salvage Convention, despite its stated environmental aims, remained a decidedly conservative instrument. While idealistic in its statement of purpose, the Convention represents an attempt to steer a course between the maintenance of the traditional law of salvage and the recognised concern with environmental protection. The Convention, to the extent that it encourages environmental services by means of special compensation, appears limited in that it is fundamentally premised upon shipowner liability. As such, any benefits conferred on coastal States as well as the furthering of the broader social interest in environmental protection is at best indirect and incidental to the performance of salvage operations in accordance with the Convention.

While coastal States undoubtedly benefit from salvors' environmental services, these interests do not contribute to the reward that salvors are entitled to, which runs contrary to one of the central tenets of salvage that salvors are 'rewarded for the benefits they confer'[1] and that 'each and every interest which has received a benefit from the salvage service must contribute'.[2] However, this very tenet is limited by the fact that salvage operations are viewed as a service owed to the owners of specially recognised categories of property, which do not include the marine and coastal environment. This precludes the proper recognition of conferred benefits that go beyond a shipowners' liability.

The Salvage Convention was an attempt to further the public and broader social concern with environmental protection through the private law of salvage. As such, there is a clear reflection of environmental values in the Convention. Nevertheless, the legal theoretical challenges posed by the significant public dimension added to the law of salvage are not appropriately dealt with. While the concern with environmental protection informs the Salvage Convention, the necessary synergies, in relation to the remuneration of salvors, appear to take a backseat because of compromise and the maintenance of traditional notions of salvage. This also significantly detracts from the extent to which the policy concerns that underpin salvage can account for interests that go beyond those of the owners of salvage property. In this regard, despite the clear environmental protection purpose that informed the drafting of the Convention, the instrument has not expanded upon the inherent limitations of salvage law.

The Salvage Convention maintained the essence of salvage law with added provisions ostensibly directed at environmental protection and the remuneration of salvors for such services. However, this system is not geared towards awards for environmental services that go beyond the linking of such services to the potential liability of the shipowner for environmental damage caused. Should one accept that the environment and its protection is of fundamental importance, the changes to the law of salvage brought about by the Convention simply do not go far enough. It is unlikely that the Convention can take matters further than it has and, therefore, we ought to look beyond the limited confines of the law of salvage for the appropriate regulation of remuneration for environmental services in salvage operations.

Chapter 5 investigated the practical and legal placement of salvors within coastal State pollution response measures and the extent to which salvors can avail themselves of remuneration possibilities outside of salvage law. Coastal State pollution prevention measures in the form of National Contingency Plans typically include salvage as part of pollution response

---

1 See discussion above Ch 3, 37 *ff.*
2 Ibid.

measures. Salvage is integrated in these measures based on contracts, often in the form of retainer agreements for tug owners to provide environmental services. In this regard, the basis for the salvors' environmental services, as part of national response measures, is the agreement with the responsible coastal State agency.

In the United States' integration of salvage contracts into Vessel Response Plans, one has the situation that the coastal State's interests are promoted, with the owner of salved property still responsible for the remuneration of salvors. Essentially, the United States' approach sees any possibility of the remuneration of salvors for the benefit conferred on the State simply being shifted to the owner of salved property with the limitations regarding salvage as noted.

The United Kingdom's approach appears to provide more of a possibility for direct remuneration of the salvor by the recipient of the benefit conferred, but this is primarily dependent on the salvor not claiming a salvage award from the owner of salved property. Where a separate contract for towage or salvage is concluded, the UK Marine and Coastguard Agency contract with salvors is terminated, which legally changes the contractual relationship from that between salvor and Coastguard to salvor and the owner of ship and cargo. This results in a shifting of responsibility for the remuneration of salvors to the shipowner. It is difficult to understand the rationale for this, and a better approach might have been for the State to retain the direct contractual link to the salvor for the provision of environmental services. As such, property salvage operations will not replace the duty of the MCA to pay for the benefits received under the contract. This approach would be a legally robust alternative in relation to the remuneration of salvors for environmental services.

Such a contract would also address the concern that salvage operations are primarily aimed at the rescue of property where salvors might claim under the CLC and Fund Conventions. Even where salvage operations can be said to have a dual purpose, the situation in relation to salvors' claims under the CLC and Fund Conventions remains murky with difficulties in relation to the establishing of salvors' intentions. However, the proper remuneration of salvors under contractual arrangements with the coastal State, especially given the primary duty under these contracts to safeguard coastlines against pollution, would provide very clear evidence that salvage services rendered were directed at environmental protection, with property salvage a secondary concern. This, however, presupposes the situation where the State brings a claim under the CLC and Fund Conventions as opposed to the salvor, who would have been remunerated for its services under the contact with the coastal State. This means that the remuneration of the salvor, based as it is on the provision of environmental protection services, can by recouped by the State. There would simply be no reason for salvors to claim under these instruments with the added difficulties of having to distinguish between actions primarily directed at environmental protection and those directed at property salvage. Given the availability of such a possibility, there would appear to be no need to address the issue of remuneration for environmental services within the law of salvage.

While salvor's environmental services and the remuneration thereof are currently regulated under the law of salvage, these could conceivably be repositioned somewhere else, albeit still within a broader framework of environmental law. From a legal theoretical perspective, this would make sense, given that we are dealing with a concern that, as shown in Chapters 3 and 4, has found a strained and unduly limited placement within the law of salvage. Insisting on further changes to address environmental outcomes within this distinct area of law could only result in it becoming uncertain and removed from its traditional reach, while also being counterproductive, given that it is theoretically not suited to such norms.

The Way Forward?

A new legal regulatory framework for the remuneration of environmental services in shipping incidents should be mindful of the broader environmental protection context to salvage operations, the need for legal certainty, and the avoidance of unnecessary fragmentation in law. As such, the approach should facilitate environmental protection and pollution in a manner that sees the components of this framework function together seamlessly. The best way to achieve this, from the analysis of salvage law and the Convention, is to provide for the remuneration of environmental services in salvage operations outside of the salvage law framework. As such, the time has come to finally jettison any designs for the introduction of environmental salvage awards into the law of salvage and to fully embrace the possibilities offered by a direct contractual relationship between coastal States and professional salvors. Before elaborating on the use of contract, it would be appropriate to briefly comment on the, to date still unsuccessful, push for the introduction of environmental awards into salvage law.

An Award for Environmental Salvage?

The argument typically employed in relation to the remuneration of salvors for environmental services is to expand upon the traditional reach of salvage.[3] In this regard, King has proposed a definition of salvage operations that include property salvage operations as currently defined and environmental salvage with its own distinct fund.[4] However, any amendment to the Salvage Convention to provide for separate environmental salvage with its own distinct fund would amount to a fundamental and radical change to the law of salvage. It would take the law of salvage beyond anything it has ever been contemplated to be. This, in view of possibilities outside of the law of salvage, is clearly unnecessary and will introduce its own difficulties.

A distinct environmental salvage award with its own requirements, as suggested by King, would create similar, if not the same, difficulties as encountered in respect of salvors' claims under the CLC and Fund Conventions. Where the salvor manages to keep the oil in the ship, would he have a choice to claim for an environmental award or would it be a property salvage operation? A single salvage operation might confer public and private benefits, which will result in unnecessary litigation on the appropriate categorisation of the salvors' claim as environmental or property. As such, the same uncertainties in relation to claims brought under the CLC and Fund Conventions will be encountered with the introduction of a distinct environmental salvage operation. Essentially, these uncertainties will simply be transplanted from claims brought under the CLC and Fund Conventions to claims under the Salvage Convention itself.

A New Approach

The author proposes the removal of the remuneration of environmental services from the law of salvage and for the exclusive use of the already existing mechanism of contracting between coastal States and salvors as the legal basis for the remuneration of salvors' environmental services. This will allow for the effective integration of salvors' environmental services into the existing broader framework of laws geared towards pollution response. Moreover, it will further the broader social interest in the protection of the environment without the tensions created by including it in an area of law that has developed a distinct property-based identity over centuries. We will have a less fragmented system and one where all that receive the benefits of environmental services will pay for such benefits.

---

3 King J, *Salvage: Bringing the Environment on Board.* Unpublished LLM Thesis (University of Cape Town).
4 Ibid.

A Contractual Basis for Salvors' Environmental Services

A direct contractual relationship between commercial salvors and coastal States can address the shortcomings noted in relation to environmental services in the law of salvage. It will provide a viable legal basis for the remuneration of environmental services and lead to a much better integration of salvage services into the broader system of private and public instruments directed at environmental protection. Where environmental services are rendered under a contractual obligation distinct from any existing salvage agreement, we will have none of the difficulties noted in relation to salvors' claims under the CLC and Fund Conventions. It will settle the question of salvors' intentions when performing salvage operations because of the separate contract for these services and the relevant intention being that of the State. More importantly, it will be based on the primacy of environmental protection instead of merely being incidental to commercial and property considerations.

Where the State pays based on a contract between itself and the salvor, it will be the claimant under the CLC and Fund Conventions based on it having paid for preventive measures in relation to pollution. There could be no doubt that the coastal State's actions would be preventive in nature, while the salvor would have been remunerated. A further positive would be that cargo owners, via the operation of the Fund Conventions, will contribute to the system of remuneration, which would represent a fairer spreading of costs across the industry.

This approach demands an understanding on the part of coastal States that a mere exercise of power in relation to the right of intervention and the right to direct salvage operations will simply resolve into a situation of shipowners having to pay for benefits conferred somewhere else. The willingness to create such direct contractual relationships with commercial salvors would be a positive endorsement of the fundamental importance of environmental outcomes for States. Moreover, such a system will maintain the importance of private commercial salvors while providing for an orderly system of mutually reinforcing private and public instruments. In relation to the United Kingdom, the fundamentals of these suggested contracts are already in place. All that is needed for future CAST agreements is to maintain these agreements even where the salvor has agreed to a property salvage contract with a shipowner and, perhaps, to seriously think about levels of remuneration that will fairly reward salvors.

Where There Is a Threat to the Environment and No Contract in Place?

Conceivably, other providers of salvage services, not pre-contracted by coastal States, might be involved in providing salvage services in a situation where there might be a threat to the environment. This would not present an insurmountable problem in that the necessary statutory enactments could provide for such a contractual link. Instead of individually negotiated contracts, one will have a statutory contract approach, which also suits this type of service where there is typically no time for protracted contractual negotiations.

Such direct link could be triggered at the point where coastal States exercise powers of intervention and issue directions to the salvors involved. At this point, the salvor acting under the instructions of the coastal State would be acting in the interests of the State and property salvage operations would be secondary to the prevention of pollution, thus also allowing for recourse under the CLC and Fund Conventions. As to levels of remuneration, this will have to ensure that salvors are, in fact, encouraged to go to the assistance of vessels where there might be a threat to the environment. In the absence of State intervention, services performed would be ordinary property salvage in the interests of salved property.

Amending the Salvage Convention

The appropriate contractual link between the State and commercial salvors will reduce the current fragmentation between public and private instruments directed at the protection of the environment. To avoid protracted contractual negotiations in the absence of a retainer agreement, the appropriate amendment to the Convention and national legislation can provide for such a direct contractual link between the State and a commercial salvor. While there might be an increase in retainer agreements as suggested by Bishop,[5] this is by no means a universal phenomenon, whilst the full extent of this contractual mechanism's ability to replace the law of salvage as a regulatory mechanism has also not been explored to date. As such, it might prove premature to simply excise the special compensation provisions from the Convention. Article 14 of the Convention will have to be the proverbial stopgap in the absence of the relevant contract or in situations where there is no government involvement in a salvage operation.

Of course, one must acknowledge that the Salvage Convention is but one instrument that potentially operates within a broader environmental protection framework consisting of the relevant public international instruments. In this regard one must also acknowledge the limitations of Article 14 of

---

5 Quoted in MarineLink.com *Maritime Reporter and MarineNews Online* accessible at www.marinelink.com/article/salvage/environment-handa   inhand-maritime-industry-864 accessed on 7 April 2022.

the Convention that is predicated upon the traditional salvage operation and that provides for a method of remuneration that fails to equitably spread costs due to being tied to shipowner liability. Remuneration outside of the Convention, based on contracts between coastal States and salvors, will improve synergies between the actions of salvors, potential claims under the CLC and Fund Conventions and avoid the unnecessary multiplication of avenues for recourse. It will also provide a sound, orderly, basis for pursuing future legal development. More importantly, it will constitute a firm endorsement of the fundamental importance of environmental protection outcomes in salvage operations.

Bibliography

King J, *Salvage: Bringing the Environment on Board Unpublished LLM Thesis* (University of Cape Town 2006).

Conclusions and Final Remarks

Changes to the law of salvage to provide remuneration for environmental services, understandably driven by the values attached to environmental protection, are at odds with the legal theoretical underpinnings of salvage. Salvage law developed on the basis of services rendered to property in danger at sea in furtherance of policies relating to the encouragement of shipping and trade at sea and the notion that the recipients of benefits (the rescue of maritime property) must pay for such benefits. This resulted in a system that would always be challenged by demands for services that involve interests and benefits conferred beyond those traditionally recognised in salvage.

The 1989 Salvage Convention, while ostensibly directed at environmental protection outcomes, has maintained the traditional view of salvage operations with remuneration for environmental services in the form of special compensation. While not expressed as such, this is arguably premised upon the narrow property-based private relationship between salvor and the owners of salved property. Provisions reflective of environmental protection values are both superimposed on and limited by the traditional property bias of salvage maintained in the Convention. In this regard the Convention appears to have gone as far as it possibly can without introducing fundamental changes that may expand the law of salvage but also negate its distinct character as a service to maritime property.

Despite the utility value of salvage operations in the prevention of marine pollution, developments in the law have not truly been aligned with an approach that views the environment and its protection as of fundamental concern. A legal regime for the remuneration of salvor's environmental services should be predicated on a view of salvage operations as a functional component in a network of measures, public and private, directed at environmental protection. This regime entails the eventual removal of remuneration for environmental services from the law of salvage, instead providing for a direct contractual link between salvors and the State as a beneficiary of environmental services outside of the traditional salvage matrix.

DOI: 10.4324/9781003315506-8

Index

For Product Safety Concerns and Information please contact our EU
representative GPSR@taylorandfrancis.com
Taylor & Francis Verlag GmbH, Kaufingerstraße 24, 80331 München, Germany